WYSIWYG GUIDE
What You See Is What You Get

THE WAY
COMPUTERS
& MS-DOS®
WORK

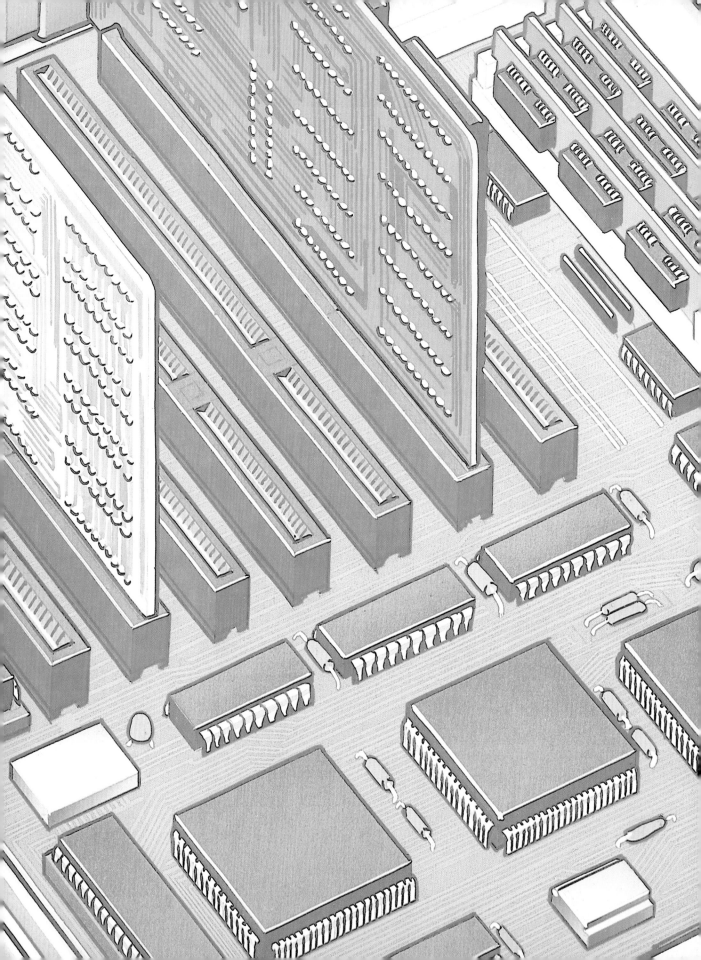

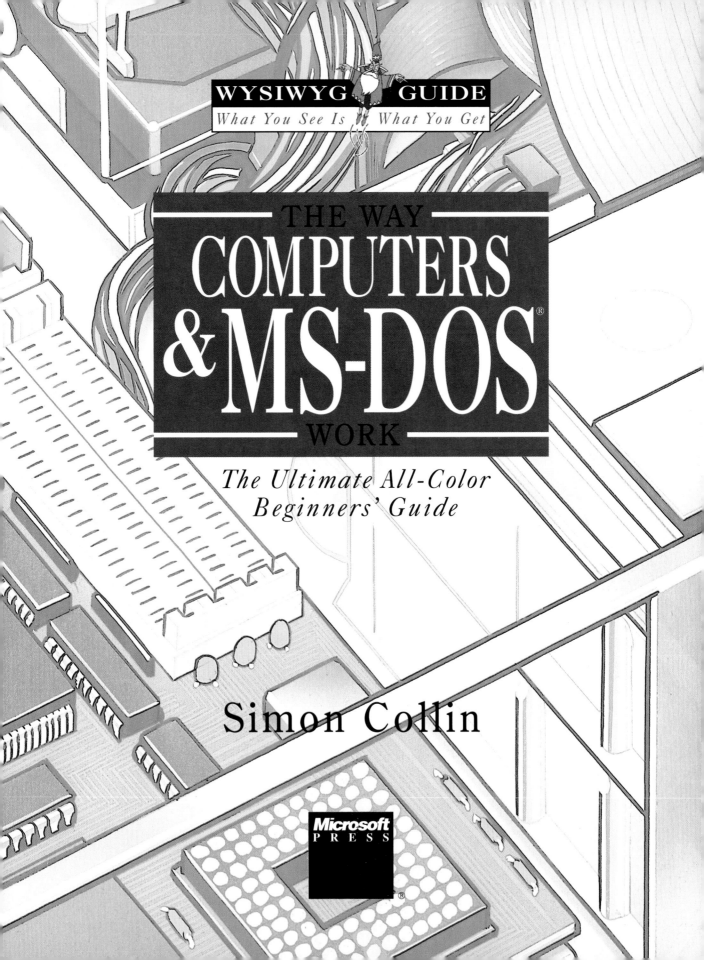

WYSIWYG GUIDE
What You See Is What You Get

THE WAY
COMPUTERS
&MS-DOS®
WORK

*The Ultimate All-Color
Beginners' Guide*

Simon Collin

Microsoft
PRESS

Copyright © 1993 Dorling Kindersley London

Conceived, edited, and designed by DK Direct Limited and Microsoft Press.

Published by Microsoft Press.

DK DIRECT

Series Editor: Robert Dinwiddie; **Series Art Editor:** Virginia Walter
Editors: Nance Fyson, Susan Schlachter; **Art Editors:** Jenny Hobson, Nigel Coath
Designers: Poppy Jenkins, Marianne Markham, Karin Murray, Sean Edwards
Computer Support: Andrew Shorrock, John Monk; **Technical Consultant:** Bijan Azari
Production Manager: Ian Paton; **Production Assistant:** Harriet Maxwell
Editorial Director: Jonathan Reed; **Design Director:** Ed Day

MICROSOFT PRESS

Acquisitions Director: Dean Holmes; **Acquisitions Editor:** Michael Halvorson
Senior Editor: Nancy Siadek; **Technical Manager:** David Rygmyr

THE AUTHOR

Simon Collin is a journalist who has worked for PC Magazine and several other computer-related publications. He has been writing for six years and has produced more than a dozen books on computers and computer-related topics.

ADDITIONAL CONTRIBUTORS

Illustrators: Anthony Bellue, Nigel Coath, Peter Serjeant, Andrew Green, Marianne Markham
Airbrushing: Janos Marffy, Roy Flooks; **Photography:** Tony Buckley, Andy Crawford, Steve Gorton, Tim Ridley
Computer Assistance: Stewart McEwen, Sam Segar; **Typing Assistance:** Margaret Little

Library of Congress Cataloging-in-Publication Data

Collin, Simon.
  The way computers and MS-DOS work / Simon
Collin.
    p. cm.
  Includes index.
  ISBN 1-55615-568-9
  1. Microcomputers. 2. MS-DOS (Computer file) I. Title.
QA76.5.C595 1993
004.165—dc20   93-13648
                                                          CIP

Color Reproduction by Mullis Morgan, UK

123456789 QBQB 876543

CONTENTS

INTRODUCTION

CHAPTER ONE

Computer Basics

et up the perfect computer system:
e'll help you piece together and un-
erstand the principal parts that come
a the packing boxes.

CHAPTER TWO

Keyboard, Mouse, & Printer

n introduction to the peripherals that
t you and your PC communicate with
ach other. Learn how they work and
ow to look after them.

CHAPTER THREE

MS-DOS Basics

Welcome to the brains behind the outfit
— MS-DOS. Find out how MS-DOS
works, and learn some basic MS-DOS
commands to take control of your PC.

CHAPTER FOUR

Up & Running with MS-DOS

A hands-on guide that teaches you how
to create and manage files effectively
using MS-DOS. You'll learn about
grouping files into directories and how
to make the best use of floppy disks.

CHAPTER FIVE

MS-DOS Utilities

Learn about some MS-DOS features
that can optimize the way you use your
PC and help you safeguard your data.

REFERENCE

Reference Section

About This Book

Hello! — and welcome to *The WYSIWYG Guide to The Way Computers and MS-DOS Work*, the first in a series of books that introduces personal computers and some popular programs to run on them.

This book is an introduction to a class of personal computers known as IBM PC-compatibles — or just "PCs" for short — and to an essential program that comes ready to use on most computers of this type. The program's full name is the Microsoft Disk Operating System, but it's better known throughout the world as MS-DOS.

PRACTICE MAKES PERFECT
In this book, we'll be starting off with some practical advice on setting up your computer system and some basic information about a PC's hardware.

Then we'll be examining the functions of MS-DOS and taking you through a few easy exercises that will familiarize you with some basic MS-DOS commands — instructions to the computer to do something useful!

As you move through the book, you'll learn how to use MS-DOS to perform a variety of practical tasks, like creating files on your PC, organizing files into directories, and backing up your data.

THE WYSIWYG CONCEPT
By the way, my name's the WYSIWYG wizard, and you'll find me popping up quite often in the chapters that follow, handing out a few tips on getting the best out of your PC and some pearls of wisdom on getting to grips with MS-DOS.

One of the first questions you may be asking is: What has the term WYSIWYG got to do with it? Well, WYSIWYG stands for "What You See Is What You Get." It was coined a number of years ago to describe programs with a special feature — namely that *what you see* on the screen is the same as *what you get* when you print it out. In this book, and others in the series, we'll be turning the WYSIWYG concept around a little bit. Throughout, the practical

Disky Business
Find out about types of floppy disks on page 24 and how to format them for use on page 82.

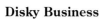

Mouse Control
How should you hold a mouse? See page 39.

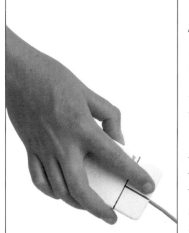

instructions for learning about software (programs) are accompanied by visual prompts showing exactly what is happening on your computer screen. In other words, *what you see* on the page is the same as *what you get* on the screen. Step-by-step, you'll find out how to get the best out of your PC and the software that runs on it.

DUMPS AND FRAGMENTS

Sometimes, an instruction will be accompanied by a screen "dump" (like the one at left) showing how the whole image on your monitor will look at a particular stage in an operation. Often, you'll see a series of screen "fragments" (like those shown at right). These home in on where the action is as you follow a set of instructions.

TIPS AND SHORTCUTS

In addition to the insights provided by myself, you'll see various tips scattered throughout the book in colored boxes. The *pink* boxes contain warnings on some common pitfalls you may run into when using your PC and software. The *green* boxes offer advice on anything from troubleshooting common problems to useful shortcuts and tips.

REFERENCE SECTION

At the back of the book there's a useful Reference Section. This includes a guide to different types of software, a summary of MS-DOS commands, and information on such topics as optimizing your PC's use of memory. You'll also find a short Glossary of terms and an Index. As you read through the book, you'll see a number of technical terms that have been italicized — these are all defined in the Glossary.

MOUNTAINS INTO MOLEHILLS

Getting to grips with technology you're unfamiliar with can be a real uphill struggle. But with the right tutorial guide on hand, the mountain quickly becomes a molehill. While this book doesn't explore every corner of a PC's hardware and MS-DOS, you should be feeling confident of the basics by the end. We hope you enjoy reading and using *The Way Computers and MS-DOS Work* — look out for my handsome face in the pages that follow!

Let Your PC Breathe!
Put your system unit and monitor where they have room to breathe so that they don't overheat.

Need Help?
Don't forget that online help is available with all MS-DOS commands. For example, for more information about the MOVE command, type HELP MOVE at the command prompt and press Enter.

1

CHAPTER ONE

Computer Basics

*Making the most of your personal computer
means understanding at least the basics of that
varied equipment known as your "hardware" —
the components of your system. This chapter describes
how to set up the essential parts and highlights what
is visible outside — including the intriguing connectors
and slots that let you expand what your machine can do.
The mysterious world inside your computer also
becomes clearer, as does making the best use
of floppy disks and your monitor.*

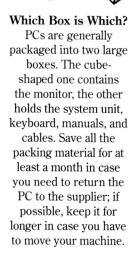

Setting Up Your PC

YOUR PC HAS JUST BEEN DELIVERED — but instead of an exciting ready-to-use computer sitting on your desk, you are faced with cardboard boxes full of daunting cables and fragile electronics. Before you can start learning how your PC system works, you need to assemble a number of components. Unless you work in a big office with a handy technician to do the job, you may well need to fit the parts together yourself.

Unpacking

Contents are easily damaged if dropped or knocked over. Make sure each box is the right way up before you open and unpack it.

If you bought your own printer — and you will need to do this unless you're linked to a printer that others share — unpack this as well and place it nearby. You will also need a printer cable. The type you require will depend on your printer (see more on page 12).

Which Box is Which?
PCs are generally packaged into two large boxes. The cube-shaped one contains the monitor, the other holds the system unit, keyboard, manuals, and cables. Save all the packing material for at least a month in case you need to return the PC to the supplier; if possible, keep it for longer in case you have to move your machine.

1 Carefully lift out the PC's *system unit* (the console that contains all the most important electronic parts). Detach the packing materials, and place the unit either on or under your desk.

Let Your PC Breathe!
Put your system unit and monitor where they have room to breathe so that they don't overheat. Don't place either in a cabinet or close against a wall — and keep books, papers, and other objects away from the area behind them.

2 Remove the monitor from its protective padding. If you placed the system unit on your desk, put the monitor beside or on top of it. Another option is to put your system unit on the floor with the monitor on the desktop.

Connecting Cords and Cables

Before you can use your computer, you will need to connect the main parts. Don't plug your main power cord into the electrical outlet or switch your PC on until everything is connected.

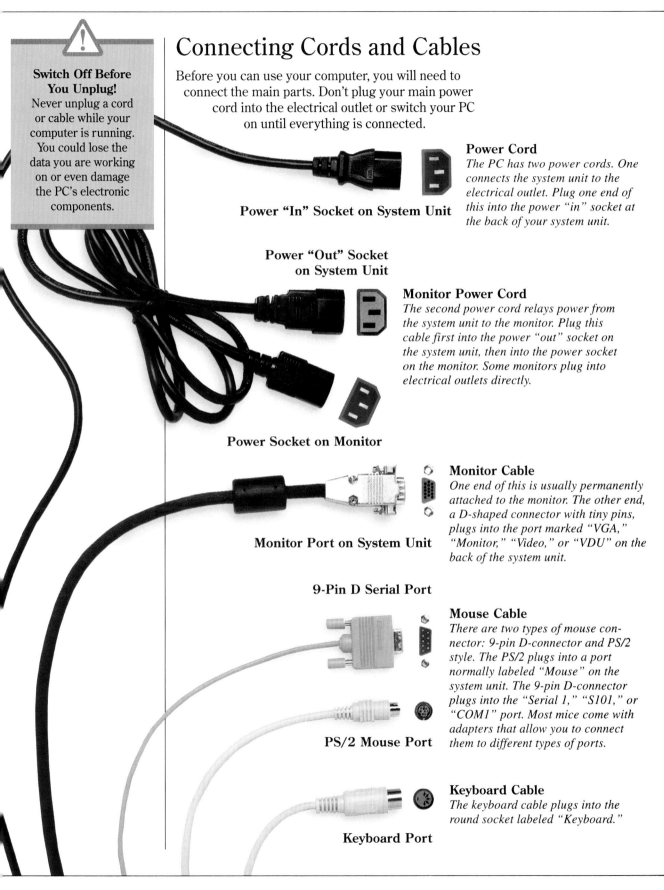

Power "In" Socket on System Unit

Power Cord
The PC has two power cords. One connects the system unit to the electrical outlet. Plug one end of this into the power "in" socket at the back of your system unit.

Power "Out" Socket on System Unit

Monitor Power Cord
The second power cord relays power from the system unit to the monitor. Plug this cable first into the power "out" socket on the system unit, then into the power socket on the monitor. Some monitors plug into electrical outlets directly.

Power Socket on Monitor

Monitor Port on System Unit

Monitor Cable
One end of this is usually permanently attached to the monitor. The other end, a D-shaped connector with tiny pins, plugs into the port marked "VGA," "Monitor," "Video," or "VDU" on the back of the system unit.

9-Pin D Serial Port

PS/2 Mouse Port

Mouse Cable
There are two types of mouse connector: 9-pin D-connector and PS/2 style. The PS/2 plugs into a port normally labeled "Mouse" on the system unit. The 9-pin D-connector plugs into the "Serial 1," "S101," or "COM1" port. Most mice come with adapters that allow you to connect them to different types of ports.

Keyboard Port

Keyboard Cable
The keyboard cable plugs into the round socket labeled "Keyboard."

Setting Up Your Printer

To produce a "hard" copy on paper of whatever is on your computer screen, you require a printer. While you don't need to buy the same brand of printer as the brand of your PC, most types of computer *software* (programs) work best with major brand-name models. Basic supplies you need for your printer include paper and a printing ribbon, ink, or toner (see more about printers on pages 40 to 41).

Printer Choice
PCs can use either impact (dot-matrix), ink-jet, or laser printers. These types vary in cost and quality of image. The printer shown above is an ink-jet (see pages 40 to 41 for more on types of printers).

SPECIAL CABLE
Printers are supplied with a cable for connection to a PC. One end plugs into a port on the back panel of your PC's system unit, and the other end plugs into the printer. There are two types of printer connections — serial and parallel — and these use different cables and different types of ports on the system unit. (Most PCs have both types of ports). Parallel connections are the most common and are also the easiest to use.

How to Connect to a Parallel Port

1 Plug the large connector at the end of the printer cable into the port at the back of your printer. Two safety clips ensure that the cable doesn't fall out.

2 Plug the other end of the cable into the *parallel port* on the back of the system unit. This may be labeled "Parallel" or "LPT1."

CONNECTING TO A SERIAL PORT
If you want a serial connection, plug the printer cable into one of the two *serial ports* on your system unit (see page 17). You can then plug the other end of the cable into the back of the printer.

Whatever the type of printer you are using, you are now ready to plug your printer's power cable into the electrical outlet.

MAKE A NOTE
After you've connected your printer to the computer, jot down the printer's name and type if these details are not clearly marked externally. Keep the details in a safe place because when you start using software, such as a word processing program, you will need to tell the software about your printer.

Port on Printer

All Ports Full?
If you already have a mouse and a modem (see pages 38 and 42) connected to the two serial ports, use a parallel cable to connect your computer to your printer, if your printer has a parallel port.

Parallel Port on System Unit

Switching On

1 Make one last check before *booting*, or switching on, your PC. You may find a protective piece of cardboard or plastic inside your floppy disk drive (the wide slot at the front of the system unit). Pull out the card and keep it with other packing materials.

2 Switches on both system units and monitors most often consist of a single button (usually at the front of the unit and marked "Power") or an I/O switch ("O" for "off" and "I" for "on"), which may be located at the front, back, or side of the unit. Always switch the monitor on first, then your system unit — and you're ready to compute.

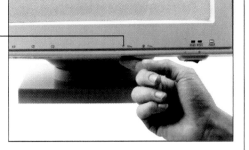

Brightness Control

Dim Screen?
If nothing appears on your screen when you switch on, make sure that the brightness control on your monitor is turned up.

Tidy the Cords
Do not leave a mass of cords and cables trailing around your workstation because this may result in accidents. Make sure that all wires are tucked away as neatly as possible.

If nothing happens when you turn on your PC, check that the power cord is plugged into the wall socket and into the PC. If you can hear the PC's fan whirring but see nothing on the screen, make sure the monitor switch is on. Check also that the monitor cables are plugged firmly into the correct sockets at the back of the system unit. If you have a surge protector, be sure it is turned on also.

Note the Numbers
While you have the delivery notes handy, make a note of the telephone numbers of the dealer and the manufacturer. Also keep by your PC whatever special support number is given and make a note of the computer's serial and model numbers.

Your Personal Computer

Y OUR PC IS REALLY a collection of separate items working together as a team — with you as captain. Some of these components are essential, others simply make working more pleasant or efficient. Adding extra items expands the variety of tasks you can accomplish with your machine. Here are the essential parts you will need, while various other "extras" are described in Chapter 2 (see pages 42 to 45).

Nonglare Screen
If you work in a brightly lit office or near a window, the glare may be reflected on your screen. One way to combat this is by buying a monitor with a nonglare screen — specially-treated glass for a clearer and easier-to-read display.

Monitor
A PC's monitor works like a television, displaying text characters and graphics in colors or in shades of gray. The image you see on the screen is made up of tiny dots called pixels. Your eye and brain interpret groups of pixels of the same color as shapes, such as text letters. Controls on the monitor allow you to vary the brightness and contrast of the display (see more on pages 28 to 31).

System Unit
The main elements of the computer are contained in the boxed system unit. All the electronic components and integrated circuits are mounted on a fiberglass sheet inside called the motherboard, which is really the heart of a PC (see more about inner workings on pages 18 to 23).

Tape Backup Unit
You should back up your data at least once a week in case something goes wrong with your PC. The easiest way to do this is to use a separate backup unit, which duplicates the information on the hard disk onto a tape cassette. You can also use floppy disks to make backup copies of your data.

Keyboard
Pressing a key on your keyboard causes an electrical signal to be sent down the cable to the system unit. The typical "enhanced" keyboard supplied with today's PCs has either 101 keys (US) or 102 (Europe). The keys are collected into four main groups (see more on pages 34 to 37).

Portables

Portable computers are compact versions of desktop PCs that can be just as powerful and are ideal for working when traveling. These miniatures come in three main varieties, called (in decreasing size) laptops, notebooks, and palmtops. Portable computers are generally powered by rechargeable batteries.

Laptop
The word "laptop" is usually used to describe machines weighing under 10 pounds. Most larger laptops have ports for plugging in a standard sized keyboard and monitor, so they can also be used as desktop machines.

Notebook
Notebooks are similar to laptops but are somewhat smaller, weighing under seven pounds.

Palmtop
Palmtops, even smaller than notebooks, are used as calculators and for managing personal data such as addresses.

Floppy Disks
Portable floppy disks, either 5¼ or 3½ inches in diameter, allow data to be moved easily from machine to machine or saved permanently. Floppy disks must be kept in a storage box to keep them clean and away from magnetic fields (see more about floppies on pages 24 to 27).

Mouse
A mouse is a hand-held pointing device that allows you to control your computer without having to type in instructions at the keyboard (see more about mice on pages 38 to 39).

Printer
A printer is essential for producing hard copies of documents you create with your computer. If you are linked to an office network, you are likely to be sharing a printer with other PCs. If you use your PC at home, you have a choice of types of printers, depending on the quality of printout required (see more on pages 40 to 41).

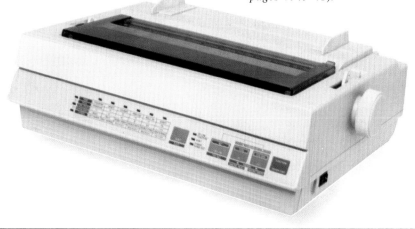

Mouse Pad
Your mouse operates best when you use it on a flat, clean, even surface. A mouse pad is a cloth-covered rubber mat that helps to keep your mouse running smoothly.

A Tour Around Your System Unit

T HE SYSTEM UNIT IS THE MASTER CONDUCTOR orchestrating your PC's operations — ensuring, for example, that the correct information is displayed on the monitor when you press a key. Connecting cords and cables plug into the back of the system unit, linking your keyboard, monitor, mouse, printer, and other *peripherals* — so there is normally no need to venture inside. The case is opened only for adding extras, such as more memory and expansion cards (see pages 21 and 23).

Shapes and Sizes

System units come in a variety of shapes and sizes, with the desktop model probably the most popular. Tower and super tower units have roomy interiors for fitting more disk drives and expansion cards (see page 23). Slimline cases have a single floppy disk drive and limited room for expansion cards.

Slimline   **Desktop**   **Tower**   **Super Tower**

Which Should I Choose?

If you want the maximum expansion capabilities for your PC and like lots of desk space, get a tower unit and put it under your desk. But if you don't like stooping to insert floppy disks, a desktop or slimline unit might be more suitable.

Front of the System Unit

● **Lights**
Your unit may display a variety of colored lights on the front panel, including power and turbo signals, and lights to indicate if the hard or floppy disks are being read or written to.

Power On/Off
All PCs have a main power switch on the system unit. Sometimes this control is placed on the outside back panel.

Key Lock
You can stop intruders tampering with your PC by using the lock on the front panel. Turning the key prevents the keyboard from working.

Turbo Button
Some PCs offer a choice of speeds at which they can run. A turbo switch is usually left "on" so the computer runs at its fastest speed.

Reset Button
If your PC "freezes" and won't respond to any commands, try starting it up again using the reset button. Pressing the reset button loses all the work you haven't saved that session, so use it only as a last resort.

Floppy Disk Drives
Either, or both, of two standard types of floppy disk drive may be found at the front of the system unit. Some systems also have internal CD-ROM or tape drives.

Back of the System Unit

Power "In" and "Out" Sockets
Cables plugged into these sockets carry power from the electrical outlet to your system unit and from the system unit to your monitor.

Serial Ports
Serial ports often connect your PC to a modem or mouse. Most PCs are fitted with two serial ports that may be labeled "S101" and "S102," "Serial 1" and "Serial 2," or "COM1" and "COM2."

Fan Housing
The electronic components in your PC generate a lot of heat. To prevent overheating, a fan at the back of the unit removes hot air from the system.

Joystick Port
Using a joystick is often much better than pressing keys to control movements when playing a computer game.

Sound Jacks
If you have a sound card fitted inside your system unit, you will see a jack or jacks at the back. These can be used to connect your PC to speakers, a microphone, or an external sound source.

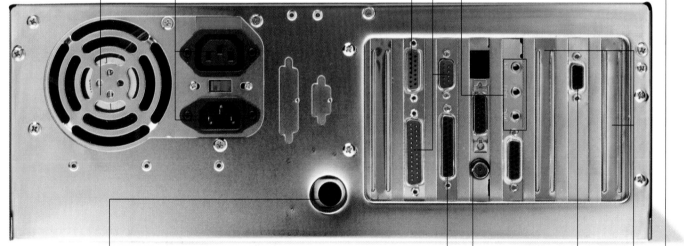

Keyboard Port
The cable from your keyboard ends with a round connector, which plugs into the keyboard port.

Parallel Port
This port, often marked "LPT1," is usually used for connecting a printer.

Network Adapter
If an expansion card is fitted to link your PC with other PCs in your office, you will see a network connector at the back of the system unit.

Monitor Port
A cable from your monitor plugs into this port and carries display information to the monitor.

Mouse Port
Some PCs may have a special round port labeled "Mouse" for plugging in a mouse with a PS/2 style connector.

Bays for Expansion Cards
PCs are easily expanded — perhaps to provide a modem, sound or faster graphics. You can plug cards into expansion slots inside the PC. The end of an expansion card (see page 23) shows at the back of your machine, allowing you to connect items.

Inside Your System Unit

T HE BRAINS BEHIND EVERYTHING that happens in your PC are contained within the system unit. Inside the unit are the impressive electronics that run programs, handle typed instructions, and determine the results. Most of the more important items are identified and described below (the exact positioning of components in your own PC may be different). More information about a PC's central processing unit (CPU), memory, hard disk, and expansion cards can be found on pages 20 to 23.

Memory and Disk Storage

One of the most crucial concepts to understand about a PC is the difference between *memory* and storage on *disk*. When a computer is running, the program and data being worked on are stored in a type of memory called *RAM*. But when the computer is switched off, everything in RAM is lost. To store data permanently, it must be saved onto a disk — either the PC's *hard disk* or a *floppy disk*.

Let It Be!

Remember that your PC system unit is best left undisturbed — unless someone knowledgeable is making additions or repairs. If you must open the case, be sure the plug connecting to the electrical outlet is pulled out.

Battery
A small battery powers a clock to keep track of the time when the PC is turned off. It also maintains low electricity to certain RAM chips that record which components are installed.

Disk Drive Controller Card
This card controls the PC's disk drive motors and transfers data. The serial and parallel ports at the back of the card link internal PC components with external devices such as a mouse and a printer.

Display Adapter Card (Video Card)
All the information your computer will display is stored in its memory. To be useful, you need to see the information. The display adapter card is the link between the PC's memory and the monitor.

Expansion Slots
These long narrow connectors allow you to plug in expansion cards (also known as adapter cards), which offer extra options not available on a basic PC.

ROM Chips
Read-only memory (ROM) chips have data written on them during manufacturing that tells the CPU what to do when you switch on your PC. The data is always there, even when you switch the PC off.

CPU Support Chips
These chips help the CPU manage all the parts of the computer.

Speaker
The speaker emits the computer's sound output.

RAM Chips

When a computer is switched on and running a program, RAM (random access memory) is used for purposes such as holding the program and its data. But when the PC is switched off, anything held in RAM is lost.

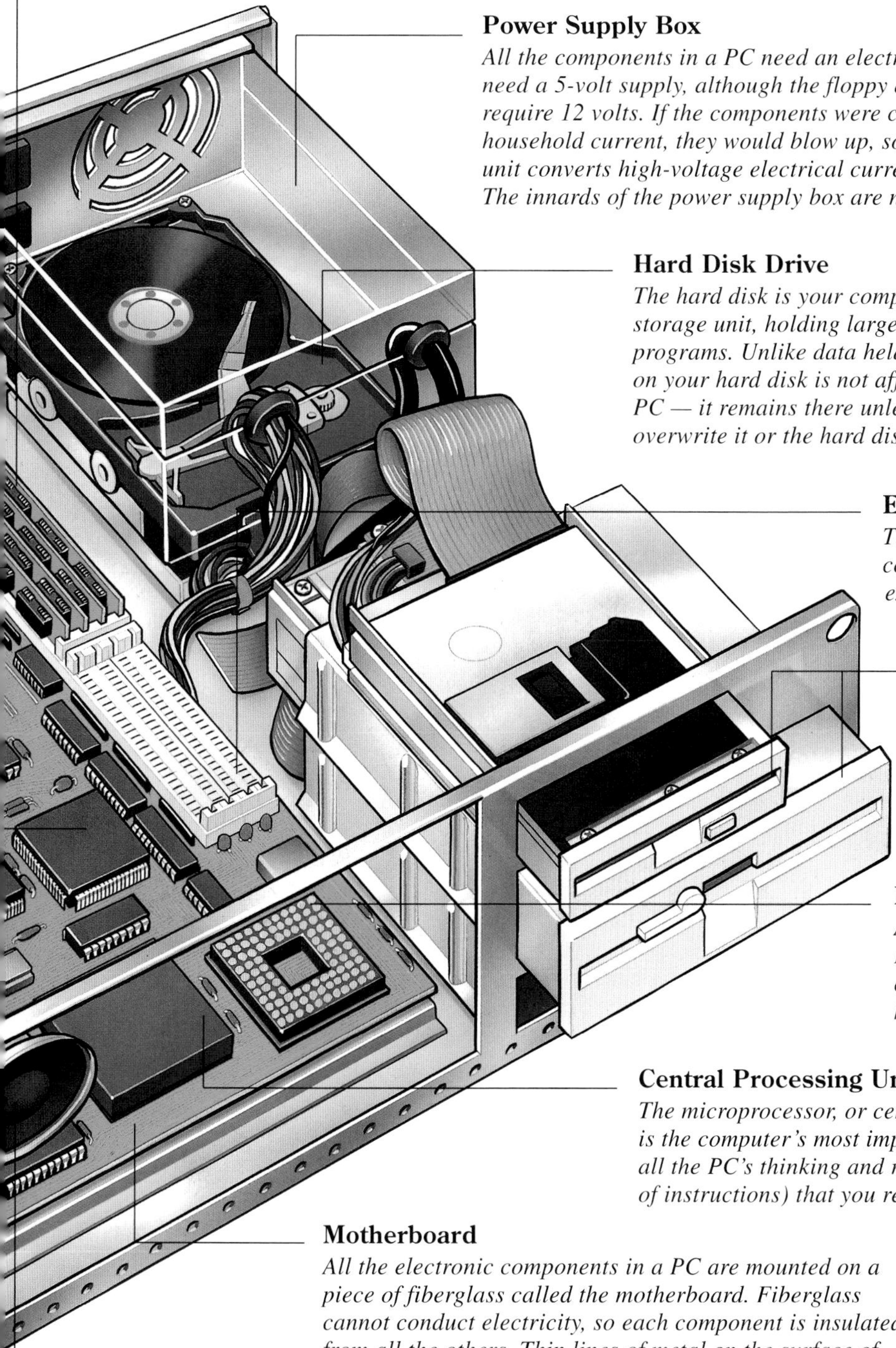

Power Supply Box

All the components in a PC need an electrical supply. Most need a 5-volt supply, although the floppy disk drive motors require 12 volts. If the components were connected to normal household current, they would blow up, so the power supply unit converts high-voltage electrical current to a low voltage. The innards of the power supply box are not shown here.

Hard Disk Drive

The hard disk is your computer's main permanent storage unit, holding large amounts of data and programs. Unlike data held in RAM, the information on your hard disk is not affected when you turn off the PC — it remains there unless you instruct the PC to overwrite it or the hard disk is damaged.

Empty RAM Chip Slots

These slots let you expand your computer's memory by adding extra RAM chips or modules.

Floppy Disk Drives

Each floppy disk drive consists of a slot to accept a floppy disk, a motor that spins the disk, and a recording/reading device that moves across the disk in order to read or write data.

Math Coprocessor Slot

A math coprocessor, present in some PCs, assists the CPU in its number-crunching activities (if programs have been designed to use it).

Central Processing Unit (CPU)

The microprocessor, or central processing unit (CPU), is the computer's most important single item. It does all the PC's thinking and runs the programs (series of instructions) that you request.

Motherboard

All the electronic components in a PC are mounted on a piece of fiberglass called the motherboard. Fiberglass cannot conduct electricity, so each component is insulated from all the others. Thin lines of metal on the surface of the fiberglass connect pins from one component to another, forming the computer's electrical circuits.

What Does the Central Processing Unit Do?

Although a highly sophisticated piece of technology, a computer's *central processing unit (CPU)* — also called the *microprocessor* — basically does no more than carry out quite simple actions, such as adding or multiplying two numbers, or moving a number from one place to another. The power of the CPU lies in its ability to carry out these actions rapidly and flawlessly. A computer program is just a set of instructions that the CPU carries out in sequence.

Because the CPU interacts with every part of the computer, a program's instructions can control what appears on the monitor and what the PC does when you press a key.

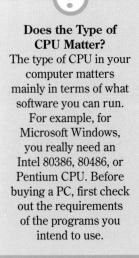

Does the Type of CPU Matter?
The type of CPU in your computer matters mainly in terms of what software you can run. For example, for Microsoft Windows, you really need an Intel 80386, 80486, or Pentium CPU. Before buying a PC, first check out the requirements of the programs you intend to use.

X 0 1 0 1 1 0 0 0

Y 0 1 0 1 1 0 0 1

What Is a Math Coprocessor?
A math coprocessor is a special companion chip to the CPU. It enables the CPU to calculate much faster and is useful if you intend to do intensive math operations on your PC. Some CPUs, such as the 80486, have a built-in math coprocessor.

THE BINARY SYSTEM

The CPU and all its surrounding components have problems dealing with everyday decimal numbers (0, 1, 2 ... 8, 9). Representing these numbers with different electrical values is difficult, so everything in the computer works in binary code, using just the numbers 1 for "on" and 0 for "off." Each 1 or 0 in a binary number is called a *bit*.

For example, it takes four bits to represent an ordinary single-digit number like "6" (which is represented in binary code as 0110). A letter like capital "A" is given the binary code 01000001. A group of eight bits is called a *byte*, each byte corresponding to a single character or letter.

PCs now use extremely powerful CPUs that can handle binary numbers 32 bits wide — four bytes at a time. For any operation needing more bits, the CPU must first work on smaller pieces and then recombine the results into a single answer.

A Universal Code
Computers may seem mysterious — but they are simply machines using many thousands of tiny switches that are either "on" or "off." By cleverly recombining large numbers of these "on" and "off" switches in various ways, a huge variety of instructions can tell the computer what to do.

Intel CPUs

The earliest PCs were equipped with a CPU from Intel Corporation called the 8088. The next generation of PCs used CPUs known by the number "80286" and were called "PC/AT" computers. Subsequently, PCs have been supplied with more and more powerful CPUs — the 80386, the 80486, and the most recent and impressive of all, the Intel Pentium.

All these PC processors belong to a family called 80x86. In general, you can run the same software on PCs containing different CPUs within this family. From the outside, the chips look different only in their size and number of pins — but inside, an 80486 has over one million components compared to the 3,500 that were in the first 8088. Because of these differences, the latest 80486 runs over ten times faster.

Another Processor Family

Apple Macintosh computers are based on a line of CPUs from Motorola Corporation called the 68000-series. Because these operate differently from the CPUs in IBM-compatible PCs, you cannot run the same software on both PCs and Macintoshes. However, both families of processors run programs at similar speeds.

The photograph below shows a typical Apple Macintosh computer and a 68000-series CPU from the motherboard of an Apple Macintosh system unit.

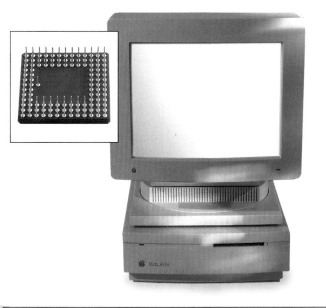

Your PC's Brain
The CPU is a large, square chip with metal pins sticking out underneath. Inside the chip is a small piece of silicon on which over one million miniature electronic components have been created using laser tools.

THE SPEED OF YOUR CPU
The speed of a CPU is measured in megahertz (MHz). A computer has a central clock that keeps all the components in time with each other; one hertz is similar to a clock tick and one megahertz is equal to one million ticks per second. Your PC probably runs at 25 or 33MHz, the central clock ticking 25 or 33 million times every second. As you might imagine, the faster the clock ticks, the faster the computer runs.

What Is Memory?

Although the CPU is the brain behind all operations in your computer, it needs to be supplied with data to process and instructions to tell it what to do. Once the CPU has carried out each instruction, it needs somewhere to store the answer. This storage space is provided by the computer's memory. If you are using your PC to type a letter, the memory would contain not just the text of the letter, but also thousands of instructions, such as those required to check spelling and make words appear in italic. These directions tell the computer to behave like a word processor.

RAM

The main type of memory that your computer uses is called RAM (standing for "random access memory"). The amount of RAM in your PC depends on the number of memory chips installed. A typical PC today is equipped with two to four megabytes (four million bytes) of RAM — enough to store about four million individual characters or numbers. Usually, RAM can be increased by adding more memory chips, a job that is best left to an expert.

Disk Storage

When you turn off a PC, anything stored in RAM is lost. Of course, a computer is of little use if it forgets the letter you've just written or the calculation you've finalized every time you shut down. Fortunately, magnetic disks (floppy and hard disks) offer a way of storing your data permanently so that it won't be affected when you turn off your computer.

Think of a disk drive as a cross between a record player and a tape player. A circular disk of plastic or metal is coated with a magnetic layer. The disk is spun very fast by a motor while a recording head moves across it. Data is recorded by sending a pulse of electricity to the recording head, which creates a change in the magnetic pattern of the disk's layer. The magnetic patterns stay permanently on the disk until they are overwritten with new data or erased.

As with memory, the amount of data that can be stored on a disk is measured in *kilobytes* (thousands of bytes) or *megabytes* (millions of bytes). The hard disk on your PC may have a capacity from 20 megabytes up to 200 megabytes or more. Floppy disks hold less data than hard disks (see page 24 for more on floppy disk storage capacity) and are removable.

Memory Boost
Some PCs work even faster because they come equipped with *cache memory*. Cache memory consists of expensive and very fast memory chips that store the data or instructions that the CPU will look at next. Cache memory can speed up work on your computer enormously.

?

Is More Memory Good?
Adding memory to your PC increases the computer's effective speed and ability to run programs; the more memory you have, the more the computer can do. However, if the programs you use are running satisfactorily, you might not need more memory.

Faster Hard Disks
Data can be written to, or read from, a hard disk much faster than from a floppy, and the hard disk can store much more data. The main disadvantage of a hard disk is that it usually remains inside your PC — although special removable types are now available. The more data and programs you intend to store on your PC, the bigger the hard disk you will need.

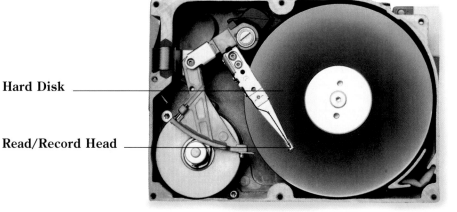

Hard Disk

Read/Record Head

Expansion Cards

If you want to expand your PC for better graphics, sound effects, or connection to a network, then you will need to install special *expansion cards*. These are fitted into *expansion slots*, which are narrow connectors attached to the motherboard at the back of the PC. Metal contacts in the connector and on the edge of the expansion card make an electrical path that allows signals to pass between the motherboard, the expansion card, and any attached devices.

You will need an expansion card for add-on peripherals such as a fax machine, CD-ROM drive, scanner, or music synthesizer (see more on pages 42 to 45).

Wrist Strap

Installing an Expansion Card

To install a new expansion card, such as a sound card, the system unit has to be opened up (with the PC switched off). The expansion card is then pushed in vertically into an expansion slot. This job is best done by an expert. When you are going to touch anything inside the system unit, it is best to be electrically grounded by means of a special strap attached to the wrist.

Expansion Slot

Display Adapter Card (Video Card)

Sound Card

EXPANSION CONNECTORS

Your system unit may have from three to 12 expansion connectors (or slots), depending on its type, but a typical desktop unit has eight. The whole group of connectors is sometimes called the *expansion bus*.

The original PCs had a short expansion connector that could transfer only eight bits of data at a time, together with all the control signals. The IBM AT bus (the next step in the evolution) introduced a 16-bit expansion connector that transfers 16 bits of data at a time. This is the most commonly used PC bus today.

There are other expansion bus standards available, including Microchannel and EISA, although these are not in widespread use.

Check Your Connector!
There are sometimes compatibility problems between expansion cards and expansion connectors. Before you buy a new expansion card, check the type of expansion connector your PC uses. Be sure to buy a card that is compatible with your machine.

Floppy Disks

COMPUTERS USE DISKS to store information. Although there is a permanent hard disk that lives inside the system unit, you can use floppy disks to store and move data easily from one PC to another. You should copy onto your floppy disks any important information that is kept on your hard disk in case your hard disk fails. Like system units, monitors, and keyboards, floppies are considered computer hardware, but they carry software (programs). Application programs for PCs are supplied on floppy disks.

Inside a Floppy Disk

Within the protective case of a floppy disk is a thin plate of flexible plastic coated with a layer of magnetic material. When you insert a floppy into a disk drive on your PC, a motor within the system unit spins the disk at least 300 times a minute while a "head" reads or writes data magnetically.

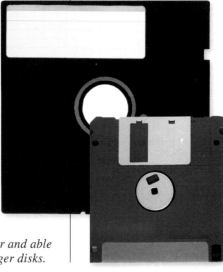

Special Coating
Disks are coated so that they can be read magnetically.

Types of Disks

Floppy disks come in two sizes, either 5¼ or 3½ inches in diameter. The smaller disks are able to store more data and are also less easily damaged, because of their thicker plastic cases.

As both sizes can be either "high" or "low" capacity (or density), there are four main varieties of disk available. High-capacity disks are more expensive, but they can store much more information.

Low-capacity disks are generally labeled DS/DD, which stands for "double-sided/double-density," while the high-capacity floppy disks are labeled DS/HD ("double-sided/high-density").

Getting Smaller
The newer 3½-inch disk is tougher and able to store more data than older, larger disks.

Vital Statistics
The 5¼-inch disks can store either 360 kilobytes of information if they are *low* capacity or 1.2 megabytes if they are *high* capacity. The 3½-inch disks store 720 kilobytes if they are *low* capacity or 1.44 megabytes if they are *high* capacity. To put this into perspective, 1.44 megabytes represents about one and a half million characters, or about six times the number of words in this book.

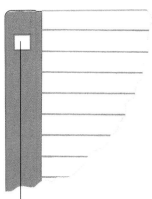

High-capacity and low-capacity disks look nearly the same. With the 5¼-inch size, there is no completely reliable way of telling them apart (see the picture at right). On 3½-inch disks, an extra hole in the top left-hand corner indicates high capacity.

Caring for Disks

Treat floppy disks carefully, and you can take them almost anywhere safely. Don't leave the disks in your PC when you finish a session. It is best to put the 5¼-inch variety back in its jacket after use, being very careful not to touch the disk surface that is visible through an oblong opening in the sleeve.

Also avoid putting anything heavy on top of your disks or leaving them in extremes of hot or cold temperature. Try not to carry disks loose in pockets or handbags where dust and dirt may get inside the containers. Don't use staples or paper clips on disks because this may well cause damage — and take care to store them vertically, preferably in a special storage box.

Remember too that you should keep floppy disks away from magnetic fields, including hidden magnets such as those in telephones, radio and television speakers, amplifiers, desk fans, and photocopiers. If you do leave floppy disks near magnetic fields, your data may become corrupted and will no longer be usable.

Extra Hole
High-capacity 3½-inch disks have a plain square hole in the top left-hand corner, across from the sliding tab in the top right-hand corner. (Low-capacity smaller disks do not have this second top hole.)

Plastic Clue
Low-capacity 5¼-inch disks have a plastic center ring that usually doesn't exist on high-capacity disks. Although not an infallible guide, the presence of this ring usually indicates low capacity.

Box It!
Take the time to store disks neatly in a proper box.

Important Cover
Larger disks are especially easy to damage and should be kept safe in their paper jackets when not being used.

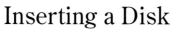

Inserting a Disk

Every PC has at least one floppy disk drive slot at the front of the system unit and some have two slots to accommodate the two different sizes of floppy disks. (PC software refers to these two floppy disk drives as "A" and "B.") You insert a floppy disk by holding it with the label side up and toward you, pushing the disk into the slot until it is swallowed and clicks into position. With a 5¼-inch drive, you must slide the disk into the drive and then close the drive latch.

Portable Magic
Floppy disks make it easy to share information between computers.

X-Ray Worry?
You won't damage floppy disks or their contents if you pass them through the X-ray machines at airports in your luggage. But don't walk through the metal detector door carrying floppy disks.

Formatting Disks

Before you can store information on a new floppy disk, you must *format* the disk. Formatting ensures that data is stored and retrieved in an orderly way. Magnetic codes that are embedded on the film divide the surface of the disk into sectors (like slices of a pie) and tracks (concentric circles). These divisions help to organize the disk so that the read/write heads can record and access data quickly. Different computers use different schemes for putting tracks on a disk, so floppy disks are usually sold unformatted. However, you can now buy some floppy disks preformatted. (For details on how to format a floppy disk, see pages 82 to 83.)

Magnetic Signposts
A drive formats a disk by embedding magnetic codes on the surface, dividing the disk into sectors and tracks (concentric circles). Two or more sectors on a single track equal a "cluster," the smallest unit MS-DOS can use to store data. The more clusters on a disk's surface, the greater the storage capacity of that disk.

Watch the Light!
You can tell when the PC is reading or writing data onto a floppy disk because the indicator light on the disk drive is lit. Never try to remove a floppy disk while this light is on because you could damage the disk and PC — and lose your data.

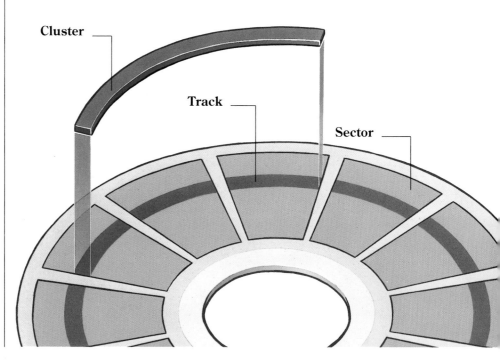

Cluster

Track

Sector

Write-Protecting Disks

Write-Protecting a disk means that you prevent the computer from erasing or writing over important data or programs that are already there. However, the PC can still read a write-protected disk. You can unprotect a disk by reversing the processes described below.

Cover the Notch
To write-protect a 5¼-inch disk, take a sticker from the disk box, locate the square notch on the side of the disk, and place the sticker so it covers the notch on both sides. With the notch covered in this way, no one can erase the contents of the disk. (You could also use masking tape.)

Slide the Tab
To write-protect a 3½-inch disk, locate the top corner hole with a sliding tab. Move the tab so you can see through this hole, and then no one can erase the contents of the disk.

Label with Care
Never use a ballpoint pen to write directly on a disk label because this may cause damage. Either write with a soft felt-tip pen or, better still, write on the sticky label before attaching the label to the disk.

Heed the Message!
If your computer shows the words "Write protect error," your machine is noting that the disk is write-protected and refusing to copy anything to it.

Disks Are Mortal

Looking after your disks will extend their life and usefulness to you. The thick plastic cases on 3½-inch disks make them more durable than 5¼-inch disks, but frequent use may wear out the surface of any disk, and if you use the same one every day it may last for as little as six months. This applies particularly if you use disks in aging floppy disk drives. As a general rule, avoid mixing disks for everyday use and those for long-term storage of important data.

Your Monitor

Monitor

Display Adapter Card

N O COMPUTER IS COMPLETE WITHOUT a monitor, the television-like device that sits on top of or near the system unit. Your monitor displays information visually, whether in the form of text, charts, or graphic images, allowing you to see the results of the work going on inside your PC.

To create a picture, three electron beams move rapidly over thousands of tiny dots of fluorescent paint that coat the inside of the screen, causing them to glow. The beams scan the whole area one horizontal line at a time at over 60 times a second, creating a persistent image on the screen.

The dots, or collections of dots, that make up the image on the screen are called *pixels*. A monitor's *resolution*, or sharpness, depends on the size of these pixels — the smaller they are, the sharper the image on the screen. An important factor affecting the resolution is the *dot pitch* — a measure of each dot's diameter. This is measured in tenths of a millimeter.

A *display adapter card* (also called the video card or graphics card) creates the images displayed on your monitor. When this card is plugged into the system unit's motherboard, the card receives signals from the other parts of the computer, assimilates the signals if necessary, and builds an image which it passes along to the monitor for display.

Matching Card and Monitor

The most common monitor types are EGA (Enhanced Graphics Adapter), VGA (Video Graphics Array), and Super-VGA. They vary in the maximum resolution of the image they can display (see far right). Image quality depends also on the type of display adapter card that your PC contains: for the best display, your card must match the monitor type. For instance if you have a low-resolution EGA display adapter card, there is no point in switching to a VGA monitor unless you also change the adapter card. Most monitors work only with one type of display adapter card, although auto-scanning monitors will work with any card.

Empty Screen?
If your screen suddenly appears blank even though both the monitor and system unit are switched on, you may have a type of screen saver installed (see page 30). Some screen savers blank out the screen rather than display a moving image. Simply press any key on the keyboard or move the mouse to restore the image.

Dot Variations
Each shape, letter, or number that you see on your monitor is made up of dots. You can see tiny groupings of these dots, called pixels, if you look closely at the screen. The clarity of the image displayed depends on the size and number of pixels.

Special Monitors
Most monitors are a standard size of about 14 inches, measured diagonally across the screen. Some specialized tasks are performed more easily using a different sized monitor. For example, book designers often use a much larger screen that helps them to work on a whole double-page spread at one time.

How the Monitor Works

If you were to take away the case around your monitor, you would see a glass tube (a cathode ray tube, or CRT). At the back of the tube are three guns that project electron beams onto the monitor screen. The tiny groups of dots that make up what is shown each contain a mixture of the three primary colors for light — red, green, and blue. The shades of the final image depend on the varied intensities of these three basic colors on different parts of the monitor screen.

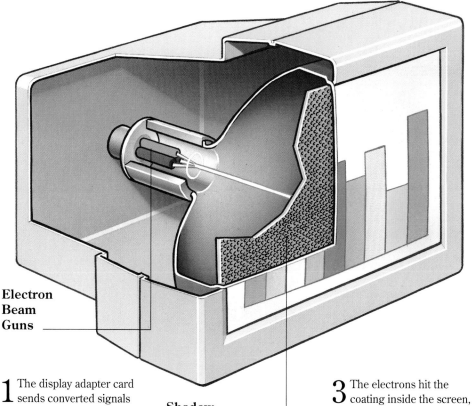

**Electron
Beam
Guns**

**Shadow
Mask**

1 The display adapter card sends converted signals to the three guns at the back of the monitor's cathode ray tube (CRT). Each gun shoots a stream of electrons, one stream for each of the primary colors — red, green, and blue. The intensity of each stream continuously fluctuates, as determined by the varying voltage levels signaled by the adapter.

2 The three electron streams pass through holes in a metal plate, called a shadow mask. This plate helps to keep the streams aligned with their targets on the inside of the screen. The closer these holes are placed together, the sharper the final image that appears on your monitor.

3 The electrons hit the coating inside the screen, which consists of thousands of tiny dots of fluorescent paint in three colors — red, green, and blue. A single group or several groups of these dots correspond to a pixel. When the electron beam hits these dots, they glow. If each of the three dots in an arrangement is struck by equally intense electron streams, the result is a dot of white light. Different colors are created by electron beams of varying intensity.

Image Sharpness
The maximum resolution of a monitor depends on its type. In general, the pixels that make up the image are smaller with a VGA than with an EGA monitor, and smaller still with a Super-VGA. Edges of shapes sharpen on the screen as you move from EGA to Super-VGA.

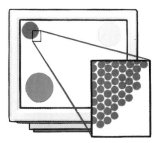

EGA Monitor

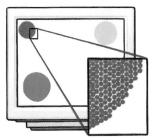

VGA Monitor

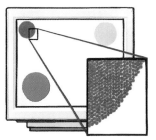

Super-VGA Monitor

Health and Your Monitor

Is sitting in front of a monitor for long periods harmful? Working with a PC monitor has been blamed for everything from eye disorders to miscarriages, but no conclusive scientific evidence has been produced to substantiate these claims. Other than light rays, monitors emit two types of radiation: ionizing and non-ionizing.

Ionizing radiation is emitted in such low quantities that any risk to health is likely to be very small. Non-ionizing radiation is a greater cause for concern, but neither type of radiation has been proven to cause any problems. Most experts agree that the amount of radiation emitted by monitors is considerably less than that from natural sources, such as the sun. If you are worried about the possible risks from screen radiation, choose a monitor that complies with Swedish safety standards.

MINIMIZING EYESTRAIN

Eyestrain — fatigue of the muscles that control eye movements — affects many computer users. Medical experts suggest that to reduce the likelihood of eye fatigue and associated headaches, you should take at least a five minute break away from your monitor every hour. If your monitor display flickers a lot, the monitor should be replaced or repaired promptly.

Some other ways you can make working at your monitor healthier and much more comfortable are listed below and on the page opposite.

Lighting Tips
In very bright conditions, you might have to adjust the brightness and contrast knobs on the front of your monitor. Display some text and then turn the brightness way up until a hazy square appears around the edges of the screen. Adjust the contrast and turn the brightness down until you cannot see the hazy square.

Keep Cool!
Monitors become very hot during use. To cool them down, hot air escapes through vents on top of the case. Keep these vents clear or you may damage your monitor.

Screen Savers
When a computer is left on for long periods with the same image on screen, fluorescent dots on the inside of the screen may become damaged and leave a burn mark. Many machines now run a useful "screen-saver" program that displays a moving image — from an abstract pattern to a star burst — if the keyboard has not been touched for a specified amount of time.

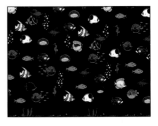

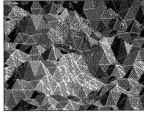

Making Adjustments

A typical monitor has several control knobs. The monitor shown at right has five:

- Brightness
- Contrast
- Horizontal Adjust (for moving the display from side-to-side on the screen)
- Image-Sizing (to adjust the height of the display shown on your screen)
- Vertical Adjust (to move the display up or down relative to the frame)

Some monitors also include knobs for adjusting color and hue.

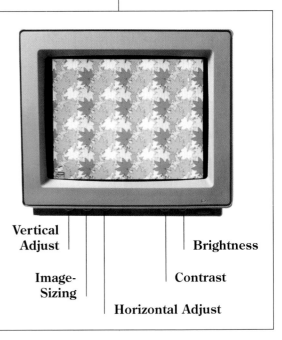

Vertical Adjust | Brightness | Image-Sizing | Contrast | Horizontal Adjust

Room Lighting

You will be able to see your display most clearly in a room that has even illumination. Use the brightness control to suit the lighting conditions in the room.

A Clean Screen

To ensure a clear display, your screen should be clean. With the PC turned off, spray some window cleaner on a cloth or tissue, then gently rub the screen. Never use a wet cloth or spray directly on to the glass. If liquid dribbles down into the monitor it could cause severe damage to the electronics, and you could even electrocute yourself.

Avoid Glare

Screen glare or a flickering screen are thought to be the main culprits in causing eyestrain. Ideally, you should turn your monitor away from any bright lights or windows that cause the glare. Attach a nonglare screen (a specially-coated sheet of plastic or glass) to the front of your monitor if it is not already equipped with an integral nonglare screen.

Monitor Angles

Many monitors now come with a swivel base that enables you to adjust the monitor angle and pitch for greater comfort. Sometimes this is made easier by the addition of a monitor arm, a special type of support that fits underneath.

Keep Your Distance

To minimize any strain to your eyes, place the monitor about 2.5 feet away from your face. You should arrange your monitor so that you look down on it at a slight angle of about 15 degrees. This position minimizes the risk of neck strain.

15°   2.5 feet from monitor

Base of Monitor Arm

2

CHAPTER TWO

Keyboard, Mouse, & Printer

*Your PC system unit has the electronic
brains to handle data — but a keyboard,
a mouse, and a printer allow you to get information
in and out of your PC. These devices that connect to your
system unit are called "peripherals," and there are others
that further expand what your PC can do. For example,
with additional hardware you can link with other
computers, scan images, use a joystick,
or even listen to and record sounds.*

A TOUR OF YOUR KEYBOARD
A MOUSE IN THE HOUSE • PRINTER BASICS
EXPANDING YOUR PC

A Tour of Your Keyboard *34*

Computer keyboards offer more than just the basic keys found on a typewriter. Discover the functions behind the special keys, and learn the correct posture for typing in comfort.

A Mouse in the House *38*

Forget about household pests and give a warm welcome to this useful input device. A quick dissection reveals how the mouse works; learn how to keep it clean and control it with ease.

Printer Basics *40*

Printers provide a physical record of your work and are an essential part of a computer system. Check out the quality, speed, and relative cost of the different types.

Expanding Your PC *42*

Take it to the limit: an explanation of some of the peripherals that will help you increase your productivity — or simply let you have more fun with your PC.

A Tour Of Your Keyboard

THE KEYBOARD IS THE MAIN MEANS of issuing directions to your PC, instructing it what to do. Keyboards are available in two main styles: standard and enhanced. The enhanced style shown below is the most popular. Many of the keys have a character or number printed on them that appears on the monitor screen when the key is pressed. Some of the keys are designed to help you move around the screen and others perform special functions that may vary according to the program you are using.

Back on Track
Some keys are designed to help you reverse a wrong move or otherwise find a way out of a mess. For example, in addition to the Esc key (which cancels the MS-DOS command you have just typed in), pressing Ctrl plus Break can sometimes stop an operation that is actually in progress. The Break key may also have the label "Pause."

No Response?
If the PC doesn't respond to your commands, as a last resort you can reset it by pressing the Ctrl, Alt, and Delete keys at the same time. Use this combination with caution because you'll lose any data that hasn't been saved.

Esc
Most programs use the Esc (Escape) key to cancel or ignore the command you have just entered.

Function Keys
Function keys offer different options depending on the software you're using. For example, you use F3 to repeat the last MS-DOS command you typed. Many applications let you find out how to use the program by pressing F1 to display a help message.

Tab
The Tab key moves the cursor along a line to preset points. It lets you indent paragraphs and line up columns, text, or numbers. In some programs, the Tab key is also used for moving from option to option in a menu.

Caps Lock
When Caps Lock is pressed once, any letters you type will appear in uppercase. This key affects letters only. For lowercase letters, press the Caps Lock key again.

Shift
As on a typewriter, holding down the Shift key and then pressing a letter key creates an uppercase letter. Where there are two symbols or characters on a key, holding down Shift causes the upper one to appear.

Ctrl and Alt
These keys are often used in combination with other keys to produce special actions.

Home and End
These keys allow you to move your cursor to the beginning or end of a line.

Delete
Pressing Delete erases (one space at a time) the character that the cursor is currently on.

Backspace
Pressing Backspace takes the cursor back one character at a time, erasing what you typed last.

Pause
Pressing the Pause key instructs MS-DOS to stop the scrolling of information, allowing you to read the display. Press any other key when you are ready to resume. If your keyboard doesn't include a Pause key, you can press Ctrl and S together for the same effect.

Num Lock
If you want to type in numbers using the numeric keypad, turn on Num Lock by depressing it. When Num Lock is off, you can use keys on the numeric keypad to control the movements of the cursor.

Types of Keys

An enhanced PC keyboard (like the one shown left) has four basic groups of keys:

■ The main typing area is like a typewriter, with keys for letters, numbers, and various punctuation symbols.

■ Above the main typing area are special keys, labeled F1 to F12. Their functions depend on the program in use.

■ The keys to the right of the main typing area let you move the cursor around the screen.

■ The area on the right side of the keyboard is the numeric keypad. If you need to enter a lot of numbers, you will find this quicker to use than the main keyboard.

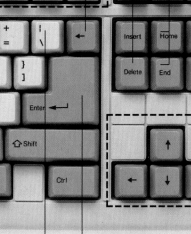

Different Keyboard?
Not all PC users have an enhanced keyboard like the one shown here. A standard keyboard has function keys on the left of the main typing area and fewer keys on the right. No matter what keyboard you have, you'll find variations in the positions of certain keys, such as the Backslash key.

Backslash
The Backslash (\) key and the Pipe key (the shifted state of the Backslash key) are used as part of some MS-DOS commands.

Enter/Return
The Enter or Return key is used for two main purposes. It can alert your PC that you have finished giving a command and want the computer to take action on it. When using a word processing program, pressing Enter begins a new paragraph on a new line.

Cursor Control Keys
The four direction keys are used frequently to move the cursor up, down, left, or right around the screen, one line or character at a time.

Generating the Signal

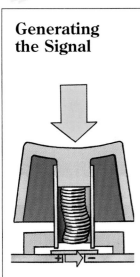

A key is a spring-loaded switch that creates an electrical signal each time you press it. If you hold a key down, the electrical signal is repeated, a feature called typematic. When the key is released, a spring under the keytop returns the key to its original position.

Spray Carefully!
Cans of compressed air (often found at camera stores) are useful for cleaning inaccessible areas of computer hardware. However, be sure to follow general warnings on the can and never point it in the direction of a person. Use in short bursts for maximum effect.

How the Keyboard Works

Each key on the board is a small electrical switch. The keys are connected as a grid and each is monitored by a processor inside the keyboard. The processor checks several hundred times every second to see if any electrical circuits have been opened or closed, indicating that a key has been pressed. Any change prompts a signal called a "scan code" to be sent to the computer's central processor. There are two codes for every key, one for when the key is pressed and one for when it is released.

Caring for Your Keyboard

The keyboard on your desk is highly vulnerable to any spilled liquid, crumbs, or even just everyday dust. If the mechanical parts underneath the keytops become especially dirty, the plungers will start to stick and the keys may not work.

STEPS FOR CLEANING
Here is the safest way to clean your keyboard. If you can't solve the problem easily, it is best to call an experienced technician.

1 Be sure your PC is completely switched off before you try anything.

2 Turn the keyboard upside down and shake it gently so any loose crumbs or dust will fall out.

3 If any keys are still sticking, use a small vacuum cleaner or a can of compressed air to dislodge the dirt.

4 If this still doesn't work, hold the keyboard upright and spray the compressed air underneath the keys.

5 Don't be tempted to pry off the keytops because you may ruin them.

Spray the Keyboard with Compressed Gas

Keep Together!
Remember that if you take your keyboard apart, your warranty on the machine will not be valid. In addition, keyboards can be very difficult to reassemble.

Give the Keyboard a Gentle Shake

Avoiding Injury

Excessive use of a keyboard or mouse can cause repetitive strain injury (RSI). This problem can occur if the height of your desk or chair does not allow you to hold your wrists at the right level.

POSTURE PERFECT

In the box below are some suggestions that will help you to avoid RSI. Take the trouble to think about your typing style because taking preventative measures can save you considerable discomfort.

Padded Support
You may find it useful to buy a keyboard rest or wrist pad that sits on the desk in front of the keyboard. Resting your wrists may help you to ensure that forearms, wrists, and hands are kept horizontal.

■ Don't lift your wrists above the level of your fingers, and never rest your wrists on the desk.

■ The height of your desk and chair are very important. You must be able to type with your forearms parallel to the floor — that is, at $90°$ to your torso.

■ Your forearms, wrists, and hands should be level. Some doctors recommend a 15 minute break every hour.

SPILL SOLUTION

If you spill a liquid such as coffee into your keyboard, the liquid may short-circuit the keyboard. Here is the emergency action to take:

1 Save your work, then turn off the machine and unplug your keyboard.

2 Invert the keyboard and give it a few firm but gentle shakes.

3 Mop up the spilled liquid, then prop up the board so it is nearly vertical, and let it dry for about 24 hours.

4 If the keyboard fails, take it to a qualified technician, who will take it apart to clean each key individually.

Prop Up the Keyboard

Supporting Feet
Before you start typing, unfold the hidden feet beneath the back of your keyboard. Many people find the tilt relieves strain on the wrists, lessening the risk of RSI.

A Mouse In The House

A MOUSE IS A SIMPLE, hand-held pointing device that can be used to direct various actions on your monitor screen. When using a program that supports a mouse, you can control your PC quickly by pointing to and manipulating on-screen objects. This can be easier than remembering and typing commands.

Mouse Anatomy

A mouse is about the size of a bar of soap, with a rubber ball embedded in its underside and buttons on the top. A standard Microsoft mouse has two buttons, but most of the time you will use only the one on the left. The right-hand button provides extra options when using some programs.

A "tail," or cable, connects the mouse to your PC. Most mice plug into a serial port on the back panel of the system unit (see pages 11 and 17). More expensive cordless mice are becoming available.

How the Mouse Works

As you guide the mouse over a flat surface, the ball on the underside rolls in the direction of the movement. As it moves, it turns two rollers within the mouse. These rollers turn sensors that send signals about the direction and speed of the movement via the mouse cable to your PC's system unit. Within the system unit, the signals are converted into instructions that move the pointer on the monitor screen.

When you click on a mouse button, additional signals are sent to the system unit that may bring about special actions, depending on the program.

Moving in Unison
If you move your mouse over a flat surface, you will see a cursor, arrow, or other symbol moving in unison on your screen. Depending on the program, you can effect a variety of screen results by clicking on a mouse button or by pressing down a button and moving the mouse.

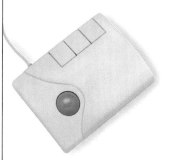

Upside-Down Mouse
Some people prefer to use a trackball, which is like an upside-down mouse. Instead of rolling the mouse around, you roll the ball itself. The whole device stays stationary, so it doesn't require as much room as a conventional mouse. People who have suffered repetitive strain injury (RSI) are advised to use trackballs.

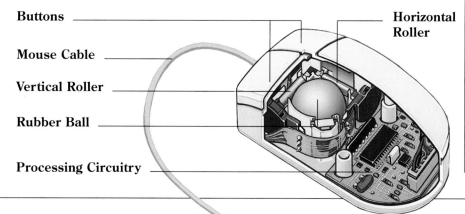

Buttons

Mouse Cable

Vertical Roller

Rubber Ball

Processing Circuitry

Horizontal Roller

When Can I Use My Mouse?

The usefulness of a mouse depends on the program. Some programs, such as MS-DOS, rely mainly on typing in commands from the keyboard — although there are certain utilities within MS-DOS for which a mouse is handy. Other programs, such as Microsoft Windows, are much more mouse-orientated.

Mouse Control

To hold a mouse comfortably, place your palm lightly over the main body of the mouse and grip the sides between your thumb, fourth, and little fingers. Your index and middle fingers should be resting gently over the two buttons at the front. Keep your hand and wrist relaxed. If you are tense, your pointer movements will be abrupt, and you will find working with your PC for more than a few minutes uncomfortable.

How to Clean a Mouse

If your mouse is not handling well, or if the cursor moves jerkily, you may need to clean the ball and the rollers inside the mouse.

1 Turn your mouse upside down and you'll see a round plate holding the ball in place. Push or twist the plate in the direction of the arrow.

2 The plate will come off, and the ball will fall out. Clean the rollers inside and blow out any loose particles. Clean the ball, using rubbing alcohol if it is very dirty. Then put the ball back and replace the plate.

Use a Mouse Pad
You will find it much easier to move the mouse smoothly if it is on a flat, textured surface. Rolling it on a smooth surface may cause the ball to slip. Ready-made mouse pads provide the best surface.

Avoid the Strain
If you use a computer for long periods of time and do not hold your mouse properly, you risk suffering from repetitive strain injury (RSI). This condition may cause enduring pain in the fingers, wrist, or arm. To avoid straining yourself, keep your arm and wrist as horizontal as possible and rest your wrist lightly on the table or desk as you move your mouse.

Wrong!
Wrist and arm held too high, which makes muscles tense.

Wrong!
Wrist and arm held too low, fingers arched up.

Right!
Wrist and arm held horizontally, fingers relaxed.

39

Printer Basics

NOW THAT YOU HAVE A COMPUTER, you might think that you can work without paper — but this is unlikely. With modern software, you'll find it easy to produce letters, reports, and charts that look good and read well. However, in order to reproduce what you see on your monitor on paper — creating the all-important hard copy — you must have a separate printer.

The three types of printers used with computers are laser, dot-matrix, and ink-jet machines. Each type accomplishes the same basic task of creating a pattern of dots on a sheet of paper. However, the dots produced by different printers vary in size and are transferred by different means. The smaller the dots, the clearer the resulting printout will be.

Laser Printer

With a laser printer, each character is formed from hundreds of powdered ink dots. Inside the printer, signals from the PC instruct the printer's processor to rapidly turn on and off a laser beam. The fluctuating beam strikes a drum, producing many points of light across its surface. Particles of powdered ink (called toner) are attracted to areas where the laser beam has hit the drum, creating the patterns of dots for each character. The paper then rolls over the drum, where dots of toner are fused to the paper.

Medium Choice
Ink-jet printers are between laser and dot-matrix printers in terms of their image quality, speed, and cost. With "best" mode on an ink-jet, you can produce prints of near laser-quality appearance. While dot-matrix printers use an ink ribbon, laser and ink-jet printers rely on convenient drop-in toner cartridges.

Quiet Quality
Laser printers are the most expensive but produce the sharpest printouts. These machines are often the best choice for people in business.

Paper Tray
Paper is fed into printers in different ways. Laser (and ink-jet) printers use trays filled with paper sheets, each fed in one at a time. You can use any copy-machine paper but you must avoid paper that has a powder coating.

Want Color?
Color laser printers are now available. They produce the best print quality but are very expensive. Many ink-jet printers and some dot-matrix printers will also print in color. Of these, ink-jet printers generally provide the best results.

Seeing Spots
A laser printout (top) has such small dots that they are not readily visible. In dot-matrix printouts (middle), the individual dots that make up each character are easily seen. An ink-jet printout (bottom) approaches laser printer quality.

Laser Printer

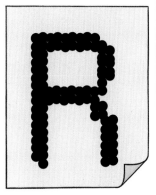

Dot-Matrix Printer

Ink-Jet Printer

Tractor Feed ——————
A dot-matrix printer can work with continuous paper, each sheet attached to the next by a perforated seam. The paper edges are also perforated and contain punched holes. When a line of text is produced, spiked wheels rotate, engage the holes, and draw the paper into the printer.

Inexpensive Option
Dot-matrix printers are relatively inexpensive but they produce lower-quality images than other types of printer.

Dot-Matrix Printer

With a dot-matrix printer, tiny steel pins mounted on a printhead are fired onto a ribbon coated with ink. The force of the impact transfers dots of ink to paper behind the ribbon. The printhead contains 9 or 24 vertically aligned pins. Signals from the PC inform the printhead what series of pin combinations to fire as it moves across the width of the page. Each character consists of a series of vertical dot patterns according to the pattern of pins fired. Dot-matrix printers are noisy because pins hit the paper hundreds of times every second.

In addition to their lower cost, an advantage of dot-matrix printers is that they can print onto multiple-part forms and continuous form sheets.

Ink-Jet Printer

Like a dot-matrix, an ink-jet printer has a printhead that travels across the width of a page, creating a line of text as it goes. However, an ink-jet printer actually deposits tiny drops of ink directly onto the paper. The dots produced are a little larger than those produced by a laser printer but much smaller than those created by a dot-matrix printer.

Ink-jet printers are much quieter than dot-matrix printers. You can choose either "fastest" or "best" mode when you print — the fastest mode being considerably more economical, producing a lighter copy which uses less ink.

Make Sure You're "On-Line"!
Printers normally have several buttons on the front. Before printing, you must be sure that the "on-line" button is selected. For changing paper or a setting, or using the "form feed" or "line feed" buttons, you must switch your printer "off-line." "Form feed" advances the paper by one sheet; "line feed," found only on ink-jet and dot-matrix printers, advances the paper by one line of text.

Expanding Your PC

IN ADDITION TO THE BASIC KEYBOARD, mouse, and printer, many other kinds of peripherals are available that can expand the potential of your PC. Some add-ons plug into the back of your computer with a cable. Others fit inside the system unit case or must be accompanied by a special expansion card inside the unit. Illustrated here and on pages 44 and 45 are some of the extras you may want to add.

Modem

A *modem* lets you link your PC to another computer using the normal telephone system. When you send data to another computer, your modem converts the data from digital into analog information, which is then transmitted over the telephone line. When your modem receives data from another computer, it converts the sound signals into digital information, which is sent to your PC. Your monitor screen then fills with information from the other computer.

You Can Subscribe
Modems can be used to connect to on-line services that provide useful information, such as stock prices or weather reports. An on-line service involves your modem dialing a number that connects to the service computer's modem.

Internal or External?
You have a choice between installing an internal or external modem on your PC. Both operate in the same way, but the external is a separate unit, whereas the internal modem is on an expansion card inside the system unit.

FAX MODEM
Some modems are able to receive data over a telephone line from facsimile machines as well as other computers. A fax/modem receives a transmission and stores the picture on your hard disk for later viewing. To keep the fax, print a paper copy. Otherwise, simply delete it after viewing. To transmit data, you instruct your computer to convert a file into a graphical image. You can then use the fax/modem to transmit it over the telephone line.

As an alternative to a fax/modem, you can fit a special fax expansion card into your computer's system unit. A telephone line connects the expansion card to your telephone jack.

Easier Access
External modems sit outside your PC. This makes it easier to move the modem from one PC to another and saves using one of your expansion slots inside the system unit.

42

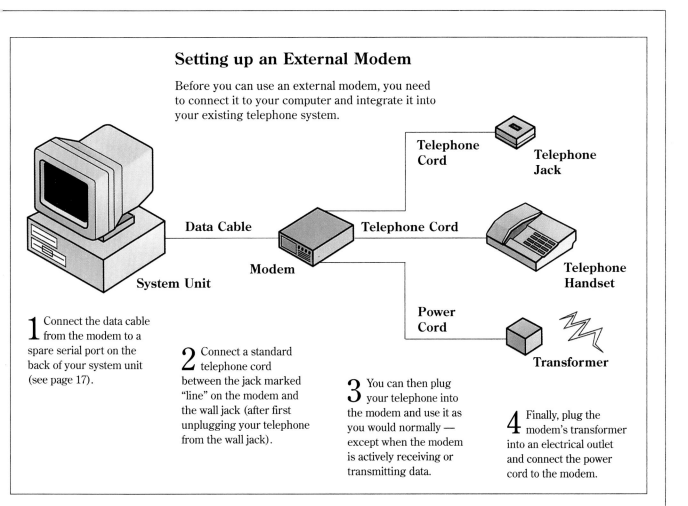

Setting up an External Modem

Before you can use an external modem, you need to connect it to your computer and integrate it into your existing telephone system.

Telephone Cord

Telephone Jack

Data Cable

Telephone Cord

Modem

Telephone Handset

System Unit

Power Cord

Transformer

1 Connect the data cable from the modem to a spare serial port on the back of your system unit (see page 17).

2 Connect a standard telephone cord between the jack marked "line" on the modem and the wall jack (after first unplugging your telephone from the wall jack).

3 You can then plug your telephone into the modem and use it as you would normally — except when the modem is actively receiving or transmitting data.

4 Finally, plug the modem's transformer into an electrical outlet and connect the power cord to the modem.

Removable Hard Disk

Most computers have a hard disk fixed inside the system unit, but it is also possible to obtain portable hard disks for transferring large amounts of data from one PC to another. These disks are inserted either into a special hard disk drive slot installed in your computer or into an external hard disk drive.

External Hard Disk Drive
An external hard drive is portable, allowing you to use your portable hard disk on most other PCs.

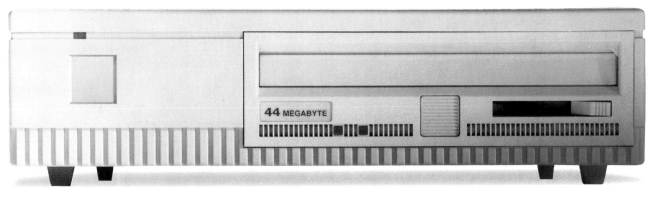

Joystick

Joysticks are the easiest way to control some movements on a monitor — such as those of the animated characters in a game, or of an airplane in a flight simulation. Most PCs are not fitted with the special port you need to plug in a joystick. To use a joystick, you will need to buy an expansion card that plugs into one of the special slots inside the PC (many sound cards provide joystick ports). The joystick cable then connects to the port at the back of the expansion card. Using a special Y adapter, you can plug two joysticks into a single games port.

Stick Alternative
As you move a joystick in various directions, the electrical contacts inside the joystick housing send signals to your PC that affect the action on the screen.

Scanner

A scanner is used to translate a photograph, drawing, or even printed text into an electronic form that can be saved permanently onto disk. Scanners work like photocopiers, moving a light-sensitive cell over an image and converting the signal into a value that represents the brightness of what is being scanned at each point. Using a scanner requires a special expansion card that fits inside the PC. A special data cable connects the scanner to the expansion card.

To convert a scanned image into text, you need Optical Character Recognition (OCR) software. This technology is not perfect, and sometimes might not be able to recognize poorly printed text.

Desktop Scanner
Scanners can be either small handheld models or larger machines that sit on top of a desk, like that shown at right. Handheld scanners are rolled across a picture, and the image then appears on your monitor. Larger images may require several passes. Desktop scanners work more like photocopiers and can produce much clearer results.

Make a Recording
If you want to record sounds for your PC, you will need a microphone and a sound expansion card.

Portable Advantage
CD-ROM drives read from discs that are durable and easily transported.

CD-ROM Drive

The hard disk inside your PC can store tens of millions of characters of data, but today discs with an even higher storage capacity are available. *CD-ROM* discs can each hold several hundred million characters of data — enough to store hundreds of thousands of pages of typed text, thousands of images, hours of sound, or a mixture of these media. To use these discs, you need a CD-ROM drive.

The information is recorded during the disc's manufacture; at this time, you cannot record your own data onto a CD-ROM disc. However, you can play a variety of CD-ROM discs in a CD-ROM drive in the same way that you use a floppy disk drive for reading from different floppy disks.

Bigger Storage
CD-ROM discs are faster and have more storage capacity than floppy disks. However, the storage is "read-only," meaning it can't be written to.

Sound System

Many PCs let you add sound to your work by installing a sound card. With the aid of a microphone, you can have fun adding anything from verbal warnings that sound if you press the Delete key to a fanfare that plays rewardingly when you finish a task of work. To hear these sounds, you can either buy separate speakers for your PC or you can use cables to connect your stereo unit to the sound card.

If you put speakers on your desk to make use of these sound cards, remember that speakers contain hidden magnets. Any floppy disks that are placed nearby may lose their information.

Hear Your Work
To hear sound from your PC, you must attach speakers to the sound card's output.

Number Translation

Sound cards play digital audio — sounds that have been converted into a line of numbers. (Ordinary compact discs use this digital audio as well.) Digital sounds can be stored on a PC's hard disk, but they take up a great deal of space, so most digitized sounds stored on disks are deliberately kept very short.

Sound Card

What Is Multimedia?
Multimedia refers to the presentation or storage of information in a combination of different forms — usually graphics, text, sound, and animation. Multimedia software — which includes various types of games and educational packages — requires very large amounts of disk storage space, so is most often supplied on CD-ROM discs. To make use of multimedia products on CD-ROM, you will need a PC that conforms to the Multimedia PC (MPC) specification, together with a CD-ROM drive and a sound card.

Can I Play CDs?
Ordinary music CDs can sometimes be played in a CD-ROM drive, but capabilities vary from system to system. Check your CD-ROM disc drive documentation for details.

3

MS-DOS Basics

*This chapter introduces you to MS-DOS —
the operating system that controls your computer's
hardware. MS-DOS is special software that tells the
computer's processor what to do when you type in different
commands. You'll find out how MS-DOS organizes the
storage of information on your hard or floppy disk
and you'll practice some simple commands
to put MS-DOS to work.*

WHAT DOES MS-DOS DO?
START UP • AT THE COMMAND PROMPT
WHAT IS ON YOUR DISK?
SHUT DOWN

What Does MS-DOS Do? 48

Welcome to the world of software, the special instructions that tell your computer what to do. Discover MS-DOS, the program that runs your PC and makes it understand commands.

Start Up 50

An explanation of the curious information that flashes across your screen when you hit the power switch. Meet the cryptic characters that make up the command prompt.

At the Command Prompt 52

Now for some hands-on experience. This close encounter with the MS-DOS command prompt guides you through your first experience of typing in commands.

What Is on Your Disk? 56

A detailed guide to the methods MS-DOS uses to store information on a PC. Find out exactly what files and directories are on your hard disk or a floppy disk.

Shut Down 64

Switching off a PC involves more than simply hitting the "off" button; learn the correct procedure, and discover how to reset your machine if it "crashes."

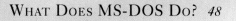

What Does MS-DOS Do?

I**N THE PREVIOUS TWO CHAPTERS,** we described your PC's hardware — the mechanical and electronic components that you can see and touch. To make your hardware do something useful, you need software, also known as programs. Software consists of thousands of instructions that tell your hardware how to behave in response to your commands. Software comes in many forms, such as word processing, spreadsheet, and graphics programs.

To use these specific categories of software (called *applications*), your PC also needs a program to link you with your hardware and the applications you use. This special program is called an *operating system*.

Easy MS-DOS It

For PCs, the most popular operating system is *MS-DOS* — an acronym for Microsoft Disk Operating System. MS-DOS is stored on disk and runs automatically every time you switch on your PC. It retrieves and saves data on disks and performs many other tasks.

File of Facts
MS-DOS saves information on disk in *files*. Files can contain any type of data, from the text of a letter to a picture. Programs are also stored as files.

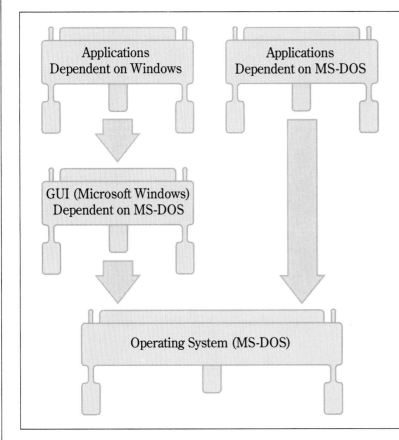

Applications Dependent on Windows

Applications Dependent on MS-DOS

GUI (Microsoft Windows) Dependent on MS-DOS

Operating System (MS-DOS)

Types of PC Software

Certain software categories rely on other types of software to help them work.

■ Applications software: These programs come in various forms, such as word processing, database, spreadsheet, and desktop publishing packages.

■ *Graphical User Interface* (GUI): A GUI uses pictures and symbols on the screen to help the user control the computer in an intuitive way rather than by typing in commands. The best known GUI for PCs is Microsoft *Windows*. This program works between Windows applications and MS-DOS, providing a means to run those applications.

■ Operating System: The operating system — MS-DOS on most PCs — controls and manages the computer's hardware and provides a link between you, the hardware, and the applications you use. MS-DOS can be used to perform a variety of tasks in the management of your PC system, although for certain activities you will need more sophisticated software.

MS-DOS Is the Link

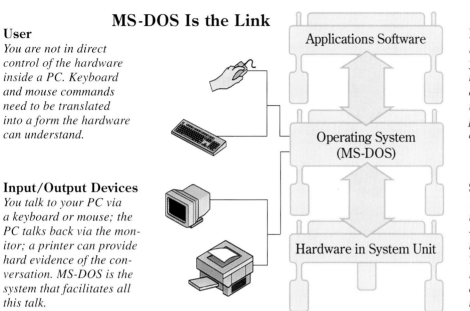

User
You are not in direct control of the hardware inside a PC. Keyboard and mouse commands need to be translated into a form the hardware can understand.

Input/Output Devices
You talk to your PC via a keyboard or mouse; the PC talks back via the monitor; a printer can provide hard evidence of the conversation. MS-DOS is the system that facilitates all this talk.

Applications Software

Operating System
(MS-DOS)

Hardware in System Unit

MS-DOS
MS-DOS links you with your PC: you type commands in at the keyboard and MS-DOS translates these into signals that the processor can understand and act upon.

System Unit Hardware
Your system unit contains the real brains of your PC — the central processing unit, hard disk, and so on. These are directed by MS-DOS, which, in turn, is directed by the commands you type in at the keyboard.

MS-DOS Functions

Tasks You Can Get MS-DOS to Do: **Tasks MS-DOS Does Automatically:**

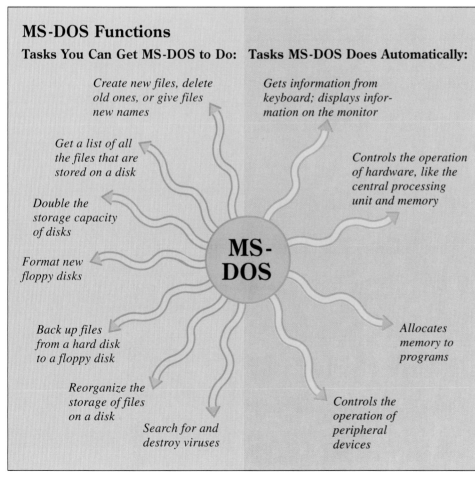

Create new files, delete old ones, or give files new names

Get a list of all the files that are stored on a disk

Double the storage capacity of disks

Format new floppy disks

Back up files from a hard disk to a floppy disk

Reorganize the storage of files on a disk

Search for and destroy viruses

Gets information from keyboard; displays information on the monitor

Controls the operation of hardware, like the central processing unit and memory

MS-DOS

Allocates memory to programs

Controls the operation of peripheral devices

Where Does Software Come From?
Software is usually distributed on floppy disks. Most people then transfer, or install, the software onto their hard disk. Some software, such as MS-DOS, is pre-installed on your hard disk by the manufacturer. MS-DOS is updated periodically, and you can get the newest version from your computer's manufacturer.

Start Up

THE FIRST THING THAT HAPPENS WHEN you switch on your PC is that the power supply channels electricity to all the components. The PC then automatically tests itself to check that the memory, disk drives, and ports are working. Once this self-test is over, it loads MS-DOS from the hard disk. Your PC is then ready to use.

A Testing Time

When it does a self-test, the first thing your machine looks through is its memory — the RAM chips — to make sure that they are all working correctly. Look at the screen when you first switch on and you will see it counting up this memory in kilobytes (KB). In the screen shown on the right, 8064KB of memory has been counted. Once the memory check is complete, the PC tests its other major components. Some machines display information on their screens as each component is checked; others report only errors.

```
VGA-BIOS (C)1989 American Megatrends Inc.

1 M Option
Revision level 1.9.F2
ROM BIOS (C)1990 American Megatrends Inc.,

008064 KB OK

WAIT......




(C) American Megatrends Inc.,
30-0200-DF1128-00101111-070791-SISAUTO-H
```

Boot-Up
The process of switching on a PC is known as the boot-up, or booting, and it comes from the phrase "lift yourself up by your bootstraps." Booting up simply means that the PC wakes up all of its components and loads the operating system — MS-DOS — so that you can begin working.

THE MACHINE BEEPS
If a problem occurs with any of these components, the machine displays a message on screen, beeps twice, and normally will not continue until the problem has been fixed. If your PC is working correctly, once it has finished its memory count and component check, it beeps once to let you know that all's well.

Component Check
As you can see by the arrows, once your PC has finished checking its memory, it moves on to test all its other major components. For example, it checks the size and type of the hard disk drive, the expansion cards that have been installed, and the ports to see what is attached to the machine.

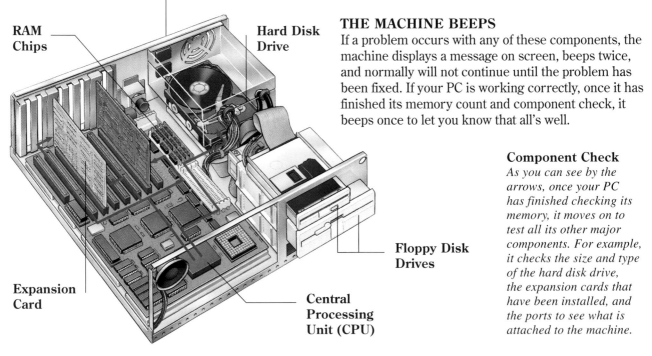

RAM Chips

Hard Disk Drive

Floppy Disk Drives

Expansion Card

Central Processing Unit (CPU)

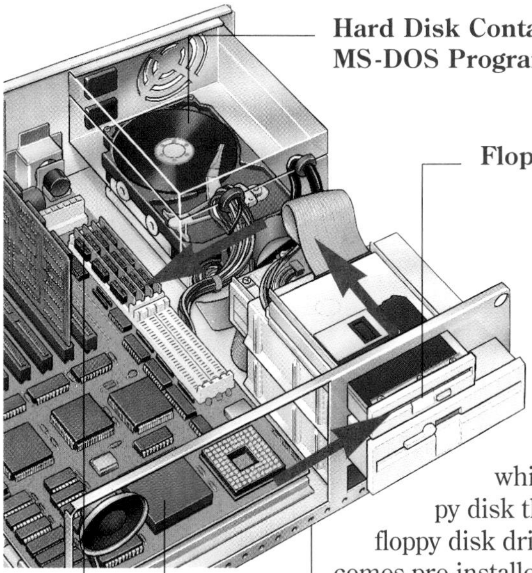

Hard Disk Containing MS-DOS Program Files
Floppy Disk Drive A
RAM Chips
CPU

Looking for MS-DOS
The PC first looks for MS-DOS in floppy disk drive A. If it doesn't find a disk with MS-DOS on it there, it looks in the hard disk. MS-DOS is then loaded into the PC's RAM chips (memory) from there.

> **Memory Error!**
> If MS-DOS displays a memory error message (often called a memory parity error) when your PC does its self-test, it means that one of your RAM chips is not working properly. Call in a technician.

Locating MS-DOS

Your PC's last task during the self-test is to load the operating system, which in the past was supplied on a floppy disk that you had to insert into the primary floppy disk drive. These days, MS-DOS usually comes pre-installed on the hard disk, but your PC will still first search for it in the floppy disk drive called drive A. If the computer does not find it there, it looks for it on the hard disk and if it finds MS-DOS, it loads the MS-DOS program files into memory. After loading is complete, MS-DOS takes over and displays a *command prompt,* indicating it is ready for action.

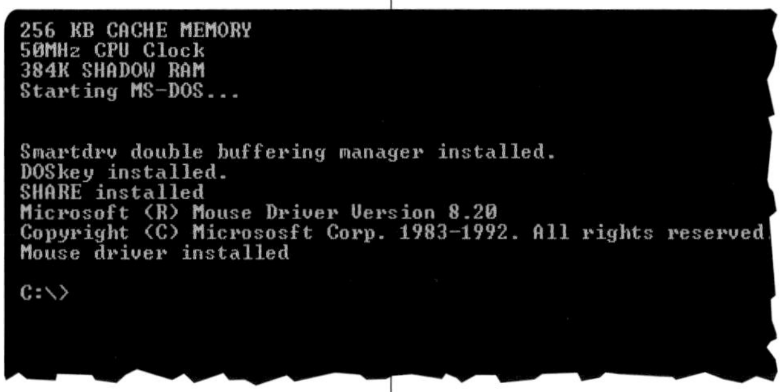

256 KB CACHE MEMORY
50MHz CPU Clock
384K SHADOW RAM
Starting MS-DOS...
Smartdrv double buffering manager installed.
DOSkey installed.
SHARE installed
Microsoft (R) Mouse Driver Version 8.20
Copyright (C) Micrososft Corp. 1983-1992. All rights reserved
Mouse driver installed
C:\>

THE COMMAND PROMPT

The screen may now look something like the one shown above right (the actual contents of the screen at this point will vary from one computer to another). The command prompt is the four character pattern (C:\>) at the bottom of the screen. Some PCs are set up to take you straight from MS-DOS into a GUI (graphical user interface), such as Microsoft Windows, or into an application, such as a word processing program.

Disk Error

When the computer looks for MS-DOS, it checks floppy disk drive A first. If the disk in that drive does not contain MS-DOS, the system will display an error message, like the one shown at right. If this happens, eject the floppy disk from the drive, press any key, and the PC will move on to search the hard disk for MS-DOS and load it from there.

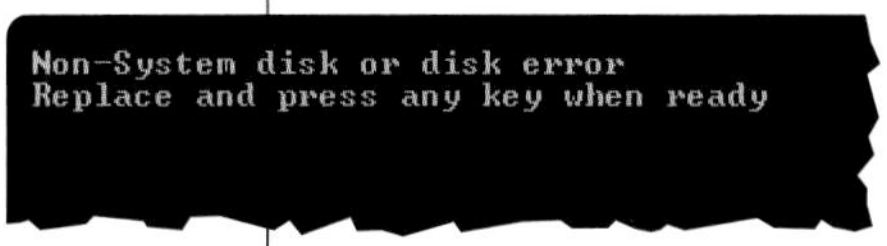

Non-System disk or disk error
Replace and press any key when ready

At The Command Prompt

THE COMMAND PROMPT IS YOUR ROUTE to the power of MS-DOS. You type all MS-DOS commands at this prompt; to put a command into action, you press the Enter key. The most common appearance of the command prompt is shown below (you might see only C> on your screen). The first character tells you which disk drive is currently active. MS-DOS normally refers to the hard disk drive as drive C; the floppy disk drives are referred to as A and B. This drive letter is generally followed by a colon, a backslash, the "greater than" character (>), and a flashing cursor.

The Command Prompt
You type in commands after these four cryptic characters. Sometimes your prompt may look different from the above, for example if your current directory is not the root directory (see pages 57 and 59).

If your PC is connected to a network, you might have extra drives available; these can be named after any other letter, up to Z. You'll soon find it easy to move among the various disk drives. (For instructions, see "Changing Drives" on page 63.)

Two Tracks

There are two ways of using MS-DOS. The first and most popular method is to type in *commands* at the command prompt. You'll have to remember a few important commands, but once you get used to them you'll find typing at the prompt quick and easy.

The second way is to use a program that displays the contents of your disks visually, together with menus of some MS-DOS commands. You don't have to remember the names of the commands, but you still have to remember how to use them properly. (You can learn about this menu interface, called the MS-DOS Shell, on pages 92 to 97.)

The Command Line

The string of characters you type in after the command prompt is called the *command line*. A command entered at the prompt could be an instruction to run a program or a request for MS-DOS to do something with a file. Once you've typed in a command, you tell MS-DOS to go to work by pressing the Enter key.

Capitalization doesn't matter to MS-DOS. You can type the command all in lowercase, in uppercase, or a mix — it'll have the same meaning. What does matter is the order in which you type the parts of a command and the spaces between them. We'll look at some of the most useful commands over the next few pages.

What if I Mistype?
If you make a typing error, you can use the Left direction key to move back through the line and the Backspace key to erase the mistyped character.

Prompt and Ceremony!
It is possible to change the look of the command prompt by using the PROMPT command (see page 122). However, for the moment you can leave the prompt as it is. If your prompt appears as C> instead of C:\>, it doesn't matter for now.

No Response from the Keyboard?
If you try typing something in at the command prompt and nothing appears on the screen, the most likely explanation is that the key lock (see page 16) is turned on.
Find the key and turn it in the lock to activate the keyboard.

Clear Your Screen

If at any time you want to remove the information displayed on your monitor, you can instruct MS-DOS to clear your screen.

```
Smartdrv double buffering manager installed.
DOSkey installed.
SHARE installed
Microsoft (R) Mouse Driver Version 8.20
Copyright (C) Micrososft Corp. 1983-1992. All rights
Mouse driver installed

C:\>CLS
```

1 Type in your first MS-DOS command, CLS (the letters stand for Clear Screen) at the command prompt.

2 Press Enter. The screen will clear and you'll be left with a single C:\> prompt in the top left-hand corner.

As you type in commands and press Enter, the command prompt moves down one or more lines at a time until it reaches the bottom of the screen. It then stays in the same place and the contents of the screen start to scroll up. If the display becomes too cluttered, just use the CLS command at the command prompt to clear the screen.

What Version of MS-DOS Do You Have?

Bad Command!
If you've mistyped a command or if MS-DOS does not understand your command, it will display an error message like "Bad command or file name." Try again, making sure the command is spelled properly and that you have not put in spaces that shouldn't be there.

Now that the screen is tidy, you can start to explore some more MS-DOS commands. The VER command (short for version) lets you find out the version of MS-DOS that is installed on your PC.

Version 6, the latest version of MS-DOS, contains a whole raft of new features. For example, MS-DOS 6 has a new utility called Anti-Virus that will detect and destroy computer viruses, and there's a utility called Backup that will help you back up your most important data onto floppy disks.

Other new features — most of which are described on pages 100 to 110 in Chapter 5 — include Undelete, which helps you to retrieve files you have accidentally erased; Defrag, which reorganizes file storage on disks; and DoubleSpace, a disk compression program that can effectively double the capacity of your hard disk. If you do not have version 6 on your machine, pages 100 to 110 of this book will not apply to you.

There have been six releases of MS-DOS, numbered from 1 to 6. If typing in the VER command reveals that you have an earlier version of MS-DOS on your PC, you can easily update it to version 6. (See page 112 of the Reference Section.)

Finding out the Version

1 Type the command VER at the command prompt.

2 Press Enter. The version of MS-DOS installed on your PC will now be displayed.

```
C:\>VER

MS-DOS Version 6.00
```

Clock and Calendar

Time Check

```
C:\>TIME
```

1 Type TIME at the command prompt. Remember that MS-DOS is not fussy about the use of lowercase and uppercase letters. Then press Enter.

PCs have a built-in clock and calendar, which are kept current by a tiny battery. When you first use your PC, the time and date might not be set correctly. Let's use two new MS-DOS commands to check the time and date on the internal clock and change them if needed.

```
C:\>TIME
Current time is 10:17:00.27a
Enter new time:
```

2 MS-DOS will tell you the time on its internal clock. The time is given in hours, minutes, seconds, and hundredths of a second, with an "a" or "p" at the end to denote whether it is am or pm. You will be asked for the new time. If the time displayed is correct, press Enter and the command prompt will then reappear.

```
C:\>TIME
Current time is 10:17:00.27a
Enter new time: 10:28a

C:\>
```

3 If the time is wrong, type the correct time — first the hour, then a colon, then the minutes, and then an "a" or "p." Seconds are optional. Press Enter and the command prompt will appear again.

Bad Time-Keeping!
If your PC's clock shows the wrong time whenever you switch it on, the battery in the system unit might need replacing. Take your PC to a qualified technician.

? Correct Time or Date?
If you've had to correct the time or date on your PC's internal clock, check that they've been updated by typing in the TIME or DATE command again.

Checking the Date

```
C:\>DATE
```

1 Type DATE at the command prompt.

```
C:\>DATE
Current date is Fri 05-07-1993
Enter new date (mm-dd-yy):
```

2 Press Enter. The date according to your PC's internal calendar will be displayed, and you will be prompted for a new date. If the date shown is correct, press Enter and the command prompt will appear again.

```
C:\>DATE
Current date is Fri 05-07-1993
Enter new date (mm-dd-yy): 06-27-93

C:\>
```

3 If the date is wrong, type the new date in the format indicated — month, day, and year, with a hyphen between each. Press Enter to return to the command prompt.

The time and date displays shown here are standard for the United States but may appear differently in other countries. In the United Kingdom, for example, time is displayed according to the 24-hour clock, and the date is shown with the day before the month.

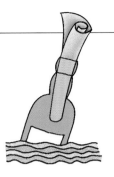

Help with Your Commands

MS-DOS 6 can help if you can't remember what a command does, or have forgotten how to use it. Just type HELP at the command prompt, followed by a space, then the command you want explained. Thus, for an explanation of the TIME command, do the following:

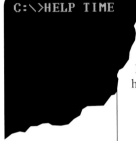

1 Type the command HELP TIME. Don't forget to include a space between HELP and the command name, because MS-DOS is fussy about how spaces are used.

2 Press Enter. The meaning of the TIME command will now be displayed on a special help screen.

3 To return to the command prompt, you must exit the help screen. To do this, hold down Alt and press F to display the *File* menu. Then press X to choose the *Exit* command.

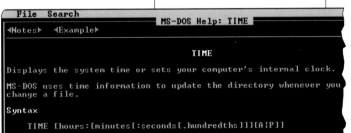

Change of Mind?
Have you changed your mind halfway through typing in a command? Press Esc or Ctrl-C (hold down Ctrl and C together) to cancel whatever you typed. This puts you back at the command prompt.

MORE HELP
As well as help with commands, online help is available with all the MS-DOS utilities described in Chapter 5 — such as the Backup utility. You can obtain help in any of these utilities by pressing F1.

Need More Help?
In many MS-DOS help screens, the words *Notes* and *Examples* are displayed in the top left-hand corner. These indicate that more information about a command is available in extra screens. To access these screens, press N or E and then press Enter. You can use the direction keys to move around any help screen.

Running a Program

If you have a program, such as a word processor application, loaded on your hard disk, you can run it by typing in a special command for the program at the command prompt. When you purchase a new program for your PC, the documentation will explain how to start it from the command prompt.

Here are some popular programs and the name you type in at the command prompt when you want to run them:

Windows:	WIN		dBASE:	DBASE
Harvard Graphics 3:	HG3		WordPerfect:	WP
Word for Windows:	WIN WINWORD		Lotus 1-2-3:	123

What Is On Your Disk?

I MAGINE WHAT A MESS YOUR DESK would be if you stored all your letters, graphs, reports, and other paperwork in one big pile, in no particular order. It would take a long time to find a specific piece of paper. The same problem exists with information on hard disks and floppy disks, and it is solved in the same way in which you organize an office or your paperwork at home — by putting similar documents together in a folder and then labeling each of the folders.

Getting Organized

By dividing different areas of a disk into directories, MS-DOS allows you to store similar documents in the same area. If directories didn't exist, you'd have to search through hundreds of files to find the one you wanted.

From Folders....

Think of how you organized your paperwork before you began using your PC — typing letters and reports or drawing images on separate sheets of paper, then putting these papers into folders. For example, you might put the main categories of letters you write into folders labeled "Business Letters," "Letters to Friends," "Personal Finance Letters," and so on. Each folder might contain only a few pieces of paper, but this system would make it easier to find a particular letter.

You might then put all your letter folders into a drawer labeled "Letters" in your filing cabinet. Other drawers might be used for reports, articles, illustrations, and so on.

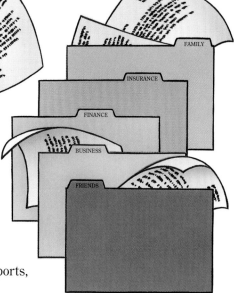

....to Directories

MS-DOS uses a similar system to organize your hard disk and floppy disks. On your PC, sheets of paper are represented as electronic files. Every time you save information to a disk — a letter, for instance — MS-DOS saves it as an electronic file, which can be put in an electronic "folder" or "drawer." The only difference is that MS-DOS calls these folders and drawers *directories*. (You can create and name directories using a single MS-DOS command. See page 76.)

If you were to draw a chart to show how you store papers inside an office filing cabinet, it would help you to understand how MS-DOS arranges disks. The filing cabinet at the top of the chart would have several drawers branching off from it. Within each drawer would be folders containing papers. There might also be some loose pieces of paper in each drawer.

The Directory Tree Structure

A similar diagram shows how a disk can be organized with MS-DOS. Each disk (the electronic equivalent of a filing cabinet) has one main directory, called the *root directory*. Branching off from the root directory are other directories, which are the equivalent of filing cabinet drawers labeled "Reports," "Letters," and so on. Just as the drawers contain folders, these directories can store other directories within them. Individual files can be stored in any directory, including the root directory. Together, all the directories and files form a tree structure. Each directory in the tree structure has a name, except for the root directory, which is represented by a backslash character (\ ).

PARENT AND SUBDIRECTORIES

The term *subdirectory* is sometimes used to describe a directory within another directory (the outer directory is called a parent directory). These terms are used only in a relative sense, however. All directories on a disk are subdirectories of the root directory.

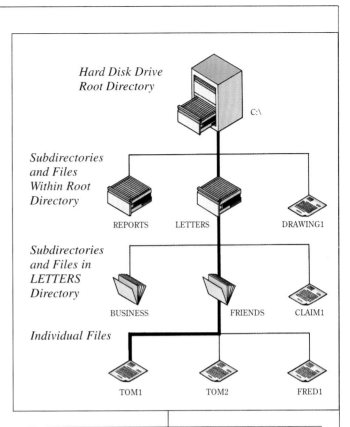

Hard Disk Drive Root Directory — C:\

Subdirectories and Files Within Root Directory — REPORTS   LETTERS   DRAWING1

Subdirectories and Files in LETTERS Directory — BUSINESS   FRIENDS   CLAIM1

Individual Files — TOM1   TOM2   FRED1

\ → \LETTERS → \FRIENDS → \TOM1

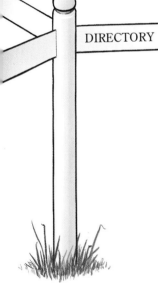

DIRECTORY

The Pathname

To specify a particular file on a disk, you have to be precise about where it is stored and give its exact location within the directory structure. For instance, to fully identify a file called TOM1 in the FRIENDS subdirectory of our LETTERS directory on drive C, you would need to define its *pathname* by tracing a route through the directory tree. In this example, the pathname would be C:\LETTERS\FRIENDS\TOM1.

The first letter of the pathname defines the disk drive. In this case it is drive C, the hard disk drive. The first backslash represents the root directory. As you go through the tree structure, each directory is separated from the next by a backslash; you cannot include spaces in a pathname.

Lost in the Directory Tree?
If you ever lose track of where you are in the directory structure, type CD at the command prompt and press Enter. The command line will then display the full path of where you are in the directory tree.

Using the DIR Command

The DIR command (short for directory) is used to see the contents of a directory — that is, all the files and subdirectories within a directory. Let's use the DIR command to see what's on the root directory of your hard disk. If your command prompt has the usual "C:\>" appearance, you are already in the root directory, so start at step 2 below. If your command prompt has a different appearance (like C:\DOS>), start at step 1.

Viewing the Contents of the Root Directory

```
C:\DOS>CD \

C:\>
```

1 Type CD, a space, and then a backslash (\) at the command prompt, and then press Enter. You have now made the root directory the current directory and you can view its contents.

```
C:\>DIR
```

2 Type DIR at the command prompt and press Enter.

```
C:\>DIR

 Volume in drive C is WIZARD_DISK
 Volume Serial Number is 1A85-744C
 Directory of C:\

DOS          <DIR>      11-17-92   1:43p
WINWORD      <DIR>      02-10-93  12:29p
OLD_DOS   1  <DIR>      04-05-93   2:18p
WINDOWS      <DIR>      03-01-93   5:24p
CONFIG    SYS      233  04-05-93   2:34p
COMMAND   COM    52925  03-10-93   6:00a
AUTOEXEC  BAT      521  04-13-93  11:25a
        7 file(s)     53679 bytes
                   65079296 bytes free

C:\>
```

3 A list will scroll up the screen. The items that contain the expression <DIR> are subdirectories of the root directory. All the other items are individual files. Everyone has different files on their machines, so the files and subdirectories listed on your screen will probably vary from the example shown at left.

WHAT THE DIR COMMAND DISPLAYS

The first two or three lines of information that the DIR command displays are about the disk itself (if you have many files in your root directory these lines may scroll off the top). The first line refers to the electronic name that has been given to the disk. In our example it reads "WIZARD_DISK," but the name of your hard disk is very likely to be something different, or the volume may have "no label."

The next line contains a "Volume Serial Number," a unique number that is useful in identifying your disk. "Directory of C:\" means the list of files and subdirectories you're looking at is the contents of the root directory of your C drive (primary hard disk drive). Below the lines of disk information you will find your list of files and subdirectories.

Slow Down!
When you use the DIR command in some directories, the list of files scrolls very quickly past the screen. If you want to stop the display, press the Pause button in the top right-hand corner of the keyboard and the screen will freeze. Press any key to continue scrolling. You can also have MS-DOS display a directory's contents one screen at a time — see page 61.

How Much Disk Space is Free?
When you use the DIR command, the last line of information on your screen tells you how much space is still available on your disk. This information is given in bytes (see page 20 for more on bytes).

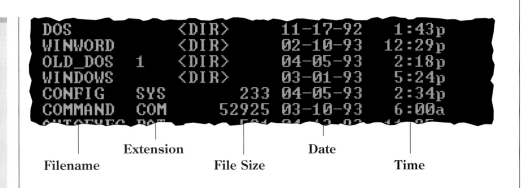

Filename	Extension	File Size	Date	Time
DOS		<DIR>	11-17-92	1:43p
WINWORD		<DIR>	02-10-93	12:29p
OLD_DOS	1	<DIR>	04-05-93	2:18p
WINDOWS		<DIR>	03-01-93	5:24p
CONFIG	SYS	233	04-05-93	2:34p
COMMAND	COM	52925	03-10-93	6:00a

What Is the "Current" Directory?

When you use MS-DOS to look at a disk's contents, at any time you are always located at a specific point in the directory tree structure. The directory you are in is called the *current directory*. To change your location in the directory tree structure, you have to use the CD command (see page 75).

WHAT THE COLUMNS MEAN

The information about the directory's contents is presented in five columns. The first column contains the names of files and directories. These names always appear in uppercase letters. They can contain any letter of the alphabet or any number, but some characters, such as spaces, cannot be used. The name may be a maximum of eight characters in length.

The second column contains file *extensions*. Extensions are three-character codes used to identify the different types of files (see below). Subdirectories don't usually have extensions; their status is shown by the expression <DIR>.

The third column shows the size of each file in bytes (see page 20 for information about bits and bytes). The sizes of subdirectories are not listed.

The fourth and fifth columns show the date and time that each file or subdirectory was first saved or last changed. (An "a" or "p" represents am or pm.)

An Informative List

The information displayed when you use the DIR command may help you to find and organize the masses of files stored on your hard or floppy disks.

Types of Files

The filename extensions displayed in the second column of a directory listing differentiate among types of files.

■ Program files often have an EXE, COM, or BAT extension. If you try to view one, it may appear to be full of hieroglyphics.

■ The extensions TXT and ASC are usually used for files that consist of unformatted text.

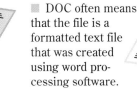

■ DOC often means that the file is a formatted text file that was created using word processing software.

■ The HLP extension means the file contains help information.

■ The BAK extension normally means the file is a backup copy of another file.

■ BMP, PCX, and TIF are all extensions given to files that contain computer-coded images.

More from the DIR Command

So far, we have used the DIR command to see the files and subdirectories stored in the root directory of drive C. You can also use this command to see what is stored in any other directory on a disk.

VIEWING THE CONTENTS OF OTHER DIRECTORIES

To view the contents of a directory other than the current directory, you use the DIR command along with the full pathname of the directory you want to see. For example, you might have noticed from using the DIR command at the command prompt that there is a subdirectory called DOS within the root directory. To view this subdirectory:

1 Type in the command DIR \DOS at the command prompt. In effect, this tells MS-DOS to open the DOS subdirectory and give a list of its contents. You don't need to mention drive C by name if you're currently using it because MS-DOS recognizes the backslash character as a symbol for the root directory on the current drive.

2 Press Enter, and a list of all the files in the DOS directory will scroll past — a long list, as it happens.

```
MEM        EXE     32150  03-10-93   6:00a
XCOPY      EXE     15820  03-10-93   6:00a
DELTREE    EXE     11113  03-10-93   6:00a
MOVE       EXE     17823  03-10-93   6:00a
RAMDRIVE   SYS      5873  03-10-93   6:00a
SMARTDRV   EXE     42073  03-10-93   6:00a
DISPLAY    SYS     15789  03-10-93   6:00a
DOSHELP    HLP      5667  03-10-93   6:00a
DOSSHELL   COM      4620  03-10-93   6:00a
FASTHELP   EXE     11481  03-10-93   6:00a
EDIT       HLP     17898  03-10-93   6:00a
FASTOPEN   EXE     12034  03-10-93   6:00a
HELP       COM       413  03-10-93   6:00a
POWER      EXE      8052  03-10-93   6:00a
PRINT      EXE     15640  03-10-93   6:00a
QBASIC     HLP    130881  03-10-93   6:00a
SHARE      EXE     10912  03-10-93   6:00a
SETVER     EXE     12015  04-05-93   2:34p
APPEND     EXE     10774  03-10-93   6:00a
DELOLDOS   EXE     17710  03-10-93   6:00a
DISKCOMP   COM     10620  03-10-93   6:00a
DISKCOPY   COM     11879  03-10-93   6:00a
DRIVER     SYS      5406  03-10-93   6:00a
FC         EXE     18650  03-10-93   6:00a
```

CHANGING DIRECTORIES

There is an alternative — but longer — method of viewing the contents of a directory other than the current directory, and that is to first use the CD command at the command prompt to move directly into the directory you are interested in.

To do this, you type CD followed by a space and the name of the directory you want, then press Enter. You can then issue the DIR command or other commands within the directory you have just accessed. You can learn more about how to create, navigate, and delete directories on pages 74 to 81.

Need Help with the DIR Command?
For a full description of the DIR command, you can type in HELP DIR at the command prompt and press Enter. Use the direction keys to scroll through the list of information. To return to the command prompt, hold down the Alt key and press F, then press X for Exit.

Get Back to the Root!
If you do try to start moving between directories, you should know first how to find your way back to the top of the directory tree structure — to the root directory. To do this, type CD at the command prompt followed by a space and a backslash (\), then press Enter.

A SWITCH IN TIME

The DIR command has many extra features that you can use by means of *switches*. A switch is something you type after an MS-DOS command to modify the way the command works. The simplest switches comprise a backslash followed by a letter or combination of letters.

Let's take another look at the DOS directory. When you typed in the command DIR \DOS, a long list of files — the contents of the DOS directory — rushed past at such a speed that it was impossible to read. One of the switches you can use with the DIR command will display just one screenful of files at a time. This /p switch will pause the DIR listing to give you a better chance to read all the entries.

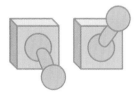

Using the /p Switch

1 At the command prompt, type DIR \DOS /p. Make sure that there is a space between each of the three parts of the command — as shown below.

```
C:\>DIR \DOS /p
```

2 Press Enter; this time, the files of the DOS sub-directory will be displayed only one screenful — one page — at a time. Once you've read the first screen that MS-DOS shows you, press any key and the screen will scroll up to show you the next list of files.

```
Volume in drive C is WIZARD_DISK
Volume Serial Number is 1A85-744C
Directory of C:\DOS

.              <DIR>        11-17-92   1:43p
..             <DIR>        11-17-92   1:43p
DBLSPACE BIN      51214     03-10-93   6:00a
FORMAT   COM      22717     03-10-93   6:00a
NLSFUNC  EXE       7036     03-10-93   6:00a
COUNTRY  SYS      17066     03-10-93   6:00a
KEYB     COM      14983     03-10-93   6:00a
KEYBOARD SYS      34694     03-10-93   6:00a
ANSI     SYS       9065     03-10-93   6:00a
ATTRIB   EXE      11165     03-10-93   6:00a
CHKDSK   EXE      12907     03-10-93   6:00a
EDIT     COM        413     03-10-93   6:00a
EXPAND   EXE      16129     03-10-93   6:00a
MORE     COM       2546     03-10-93   6:00a
MSD      EXE     158470     03-10-93   6:00a
QBASIC   EXE     194309     03-10-93   6:00a
RESTORE  EXE      38294     03-10-93   6:00a
SYS      COM       9379     03-10-93   6:00a
Press any key to continue . . .
```

A BROADER VIEW

Another useful switch that can be used with the DIR command is /w. It gives you a list of all the subdirectories and files within a directory without listing the details of file size, date, or time.

Using the /w Switch

```
C:\>DIR /w
```

1 Type DIR /w at the command prompt. Remember that the switches for the DIR command are always entered at the very end of the line, after the actual command and the name of the directory you want to see.

```
C:\>DIR /w

 Volume in drive C is WIZARD_DISK
 Volume Serial Number is 1A85-744C
 Directory of C:\

[DOS]           [WINWORD]        [OLD_DOS.1]      [WINDOWS]        CONFIG.SYS
COMMAND.COM     AUTOEXEC.BAT
        7 file(s)         53679 bytes
                       64978944 bytes free
```

2 Press Enter, and you will get a "wide" listing of the root directory's contents.

Want More Switches?
In addition to /p and /w, there are many other switches that can be used with the DIR command. For example, the /od switch will give you a listing of files and subdirectories in the order (by date) that they were created. You can use two or more switches with one DIR command, as long as you separate them with a slash. To view a full list of the switches available, and their effects, use the HELP DIR command.

61

Viewing a File's Contents

You can read the contents of a file by using the MS-DOS command TYPE followed by a filename. The TYPE command is most useful to see the contents of unformatted text files — those with a TXT, ASC, or BAT extension. Of the main types of program files (EXE, COM, and BAT), those with a BAT extension are the only ones that show MS-DOS commands in plain unformatted form. You can view the contents of these files by using the TYPE command.

Using the TYPE Command

```
C:\>TYPE AUTOEXEC.BAT
```

1 Enter TYPE AUTOEXEC.BAT at the command prompt. Don't forget to include a space between the TYPE command and the filename.

2 When you press Enter, you will see the contents of the file called AUTOEXEC.BAT, which is stored in the root directory. This file stores commands that are run when your PC starts up. We'll take a closer look at it on page 89. (The contents of your AUTOEXEC.BAT file will not look exactly the same as the example shown here.)

```
C:\>TYPE AUTOEXEC.BAT
@ECHO OFF
PROMPT $p$g
PATH C:\DOS;C:\WINWORD;C:\WINDOWS
SET TEMP=C:\DOS
LH C:\DOS\DOSKEY
LH C:\DOS\SHARE.EXE
LH C:\DOS\mouse.COM /Y

C:\>
```

Try using the TYPE command to view other files stored in the root directory. (To find the names of other files, remember that the DIR command will list all the files in the directory). Any files that appear to be made up of nonsense rather than character combinations you recognize are program files that contain special commands to MS-DOS and the processor.

Looking at a Floppy Disk

So far in this chapter, we've looked at the files and directories on your PC's hard disk. Floppy disks can also store files, which can be organized into directories in exactly the same way.

In order to look at what's stored on a floppy disk, you must insert the floppy disk in a drive, and then instruct MS-DOS to start using the floppy disk drive instead of the hard disk drive.

Watch the Period!
To identify a file at the command prompt, you must type in both its file name and extension. The two parts must also be separated by a period. For example, a file named BANK.DOC in the directory listing can be viewed only by typing TYPE BANK.DOC at the command prompt.

Hear Beeps When You Use the TYPE Command?
You have attempted to view the contents of a program file. The beeps are special commands that are understood only by the processor. The TYPE command doesn't know how to display them, so it beeps. To stop it, press Ctrl-C.

Which Floppy Drive is Which?
If your system unit has two disk drives and you are not sure which is A and which is B, put a formatted disk in both of the drives and type A: (that's A followed by a colon) at the command prompt. When you press Enter, the light on the front of one of your floppy drives will light up for a moment; this is drive A.

Changing Drives

1 First insert the floppy disk into the correct disk drive. Use a floppy disk that you know contains some files. If you have two floppy disk drives, one is called drive "A," and the other drive "B." Let's assume you're using drive A.

```
C:\>A:
```

2 Type A: at the command prompt and press Enter.

```
C:\>A:

A:\>
```

3 You'll see the light on your floppy disk drive light up for a moment. MS-DOS is now addressing floppy disk drive A. You'll also see that the command prompt has changed to display A:\>.

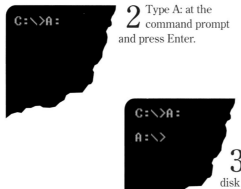

?

Error Message from Drive A?
If an error message appears indicating that MS-DOS cannot read from floppy disk drive A, followed by the words "Abort, Retry, Fail?" it means either you haven't put a floppy disk into the drive, the disk is bad, or the disk is not yet formatted. To correct this, put a formatted floppy disk into the disk drive, type R for Retry and press Enter. If you don't have a formatted disk, press F indicating you want the request to fail, then type C: and press Enter.

DRIVE A AND THE DIR COMMAND

You can now type any of the MS-DOS commands discussed on the previous pages, and they'll refer to the floppy disk drive A instead of the hard disk drive C. Use the DIR command to see the files stored in the root directory of the disk in drive A.

Viewing a Floppy Disk's Contents

1 At the command prompt A:\>, type the command DIR.

```
A:\>DIR
```

2 Press Enter, and you'll see a list of all the files (and any subdirectories) stored in the root directory of your floppy disk. You can use the same switches with the DIR command that we have discussed so far.

```
A:\>DIR

 Volume in drive A is WYSIWYG
 Directory of A:\

FLUFFY   BMP    287925 11-20-91  12:00p
BRYN1    DOC       102 03-08-93   7:48p
BRYN2    DOC      5115 05-06-93   6:32p
LETTER1  DOC      6766 03-10-92   3:10a
CHART3   XLS       500 04-05-93   2:12p
ARTICLE1 TXT      4717 05-04-93   4:34p
       6 file(s)       305125 bytes
                       907264 bytes free

A:\>
```

CHANGING BACK TO THE C DRIVE

To change back to the hard disk drive C from the floppy drive, type C: (that's C followed by a colon) at the command prompt and press Enter. You'll see the command prompt change from A:\> back to C:\>.

When the hard drive is the current drive again, you can eject the disk from your floppy drive. Always make sure that the drive light is off before you eject the disk.

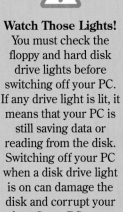

Shut Down

W HEN YOU HAVE FINISHED WORKING on your computer for the day, it is best to switch off your PC rather than leaving it on all night. But however weary you might feel, don't be tempted to just switch it off. A quick flick of the switch is fine to shut down a television — but with a PC you must follow a short sequence of steps to ensure your work is safe and to prevent damage to your hardware.

When to Power Off

Switching your computer on and off several times a day is not a good idea. Every time you turn on a computer, internal components are heated, and these cool when you switch the unit off. The change in temperature causes circuit boards to expand and contract, which increases wear and tear on solder joints.

For this reason, some people advocate leaving the system unit on all the time if you are a regular PC user. (Although many maintain that you should turn your monitor off at night.) Generally, however, it is probably best to shut down the system unit at the end of each day's work. Leaving your computer on all the time means that motors in the hard disk drive and fan housing are working non-stop, and this increases the strain on the bearings.

How to Turn Off Your Computer

If you have been using a computer application, such as a word processing program, it is very important that you save your work before turning off your computer. The command sequence needed to save work varies among programs, and you should find out what it is from the program's documentation before you begin. Having saved your work, you should then quit the program to return to the command prompt. If you simply switch off your PC when an application is running, you might corrupt (or disorganize) a file. Once back at the command prompt, you are ready to follow the final steps to shutting down your PC. This is described at the top of the next page.

Ctrl Key   **Alt Key**

Last Steps when Shutting Down

Be sure your monitor screen shows that you are back at the command prompt before you follow these last steps for your nightly PC shut down:

1 Remove any floppy disks in your disk drives. Take a moment to put any 5¼-inch disks back in their protective covers, then put all disks back in their storage box.

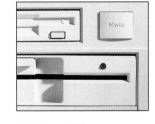

2 Turn off the computer by pressing the button or flipping the switch on the system unit.

3 Press the button or switch on the monitor so your screen is turned off as well.

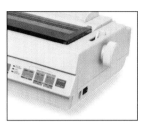

4 Switch off your printer and any other PC peripherals you are using.

Resetting Your PC

Special Combination
To reset your PC, you can press the Ctrl, Alt, and Delete keys at the same time. This combination should be used only if the PC freezes up completely and the only other solution is to switch off the unit.

However careful you are, sometimes the software running on your PC might not function properly and the computer "crashes." One solution is to switch off your PC, wait for a minute, then switch on again.

Another alternative, which is less wearing for your hardware, is to reset the computer. When you reset, the power supply to the CPU is interrupted, which causes it to restart. You can reset the computer by pressing the reset button on the system unit, or by pressing a special combination of keys on the keyboard (Ctrl-Alt-Del). Resetting a PC has the same effect on any program you are running as switching the computer off — so if you have not saved your work, use this option only as a last resort.

Delete Key

Have You Crashed?
After you've been using a PC for a while, you'll begin to recognize the common symptoms of a "crash." The display on your monitor screen freezes or begins to behave oddly, and you won't be able to select any of the options. As a first step, try pressing the Esc key or the Ctrl-Break key combination. If that doesn't work, you may need to reset the computer.

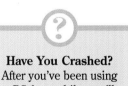

4

CHAPTER FOUR

*U*p *& Running with MS-DOS*

*Now that you have mastered some
basic MS-DOS commands, you can move on to
some practical tasks. In this chapter, you'll learn
how to handle files and navigate directories confidently
and successfully. Floppy disks can be very useful for
storing copies of important files and carrying data
between PCs. In this chapter, you'll learn how to
format a floppy disk and how to move files
onto a floppy disk from your hard disk.*

FUN WITH FILES • DABBLING WITH DIRECTORIES
DISKY BUSINESS • WILDCARDS
TWO SPECIAL FILES

Fun with Files *68*

How to create, save, print, copy, rename, and delete files. Learn about the UNDELETE command — a lifesaver for recovering files that you may have erased by mistake.

Dabbling with Directories *74*

How to find your way around the directory tree structure. An explanation of how to create and delete directories, move files between them, and find lost files.

Disky Business *82*

Formats and capacities: how to get a floppy disk ready for use by your PC, and the method for copying files from hard to floppy disk. Master the art of duplicating an entire disk.

Wildcards *86*

The jokers in the deck: asterisks and question marks can be used to manipulate large groups of files with a single command. Discover how they can save you time and effort.

Two Special Files *88*

The root to controlling MS-DOS — and your PC's set up — lies in your AUTOEXEC.BAT and CONFIG.SYS files. An investigation into their contents and functions.

Fun With Files

W HENEVER YOU SAVE SOMETHING YOU HAVE CREATED on your PC, you save it as a file. In Chapter 3, you learned something about the variety of files that can be stored on either a hard disk or a floppy disk — for example, document files, text files, image files, and program files. You give each file a name to help you to identify its contents and an extension that tells you what type of file it is. In this section, you'll learn how to create a file, save it on your hard disk, and then print it. Later, you'll learn how to change the name of the file, create a copy of the file, or delete it altogether.

Naming a File?
You can give a file any name, but remember that you are limited to eight characters for the main part of the name, and three characters for the extension after the period. A standard extension for simple text files is TXT. The space character and the following characters are not valid in a filename:
? . " / \ [ ] * : | < > = + , ;

How to Create a File

Using the MS-DOS Editor

`C:\>EDIT`

To create your first file, you can use the Editor utility that is built into MS-DOS. Using the Editor is like using a very basic word processor. You can type in text and edit it, but you cannot format the text with fonts (typefaces) or special effects. The Editor is used mainly to create short text files and modify special system files.

1 Start the MS-DOS Editor utility by typing EDIT at the command prompt.

2 Press Enter. After a moment, you'll see a welcome message with the invitation to press Enter to see the "Survival Guide," which describes how to use the Editor. Go ahead and press Enter. After you have read the contents of the screen, press Esc to clear your display.

```
          Welcome to the MS-DOS Editor
Copyright (C) Microsoft Corporation, 1987-1992.
              All rights reserved.
   < Press Enter to see the Survival Guide >
   < Press ESC to clear this dialog box >
```

```
 File  Edit  Search  Options
                      Untitled
```

3 You are now ready to begin typing in text. The main screen display of the Editor has a menu bar along the top, and a title (at present still labeled *Untitled*).

```
 File  Edit  Search  Options
                      Untitled
I always eat peas with honey
I've done it all my life,
They do taste kind of funny,
But it keeps them on the knife
```

4 Type in a few lines, say, of a poem. You will need to press Enter at the end of each line. Use the Backspace key to correct errors. If you spot a mistake a few lines back, use the direction keys to put the cursor just in front of the error, then use the Backspace key to delete it.

How to Save Your File

Once you have typed in the poem, or any other text, you need to save the information in a file. At present, the text exists as electrical states inside a RAM chip that makes up your PC's memory. If you switch off your computer now, before saving your work, the text will be lost. Saving the information on your hard disk will store it permanently, even when you switch off your machine.

All the main commands in the Editor utility are displayed in menus. To use the menu command that lets you save your text, follow five simple steps.

Extensions to Avoid!
Three extensions, COM, EXE, and SYS, are reserved for MS-DOS program files used on your computer. Don't use these for any of your own files.

Saving Your File Contents

1 Hold down the Alt key and then press F. (This key combination is called Alt-F.) You'll see a menu appear from below the word *File* in the menu bar.

2 Now press the Down direction key to move the highlight bar down the menu until it reaches the *Save As* option.

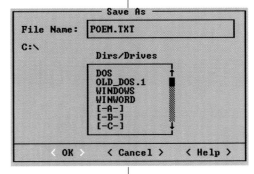

3 Press Enter. The menu disappears, and a dialog box now appears on screen. In the *File Name* box, type in the name you want to call the file (for example, POEM.TXT).

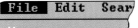

4 Press Enter. The box disappears, the file is saved, and you are back at the main screen. Look at the hard disk drive light when you save the file. This light should remain on for a few seconds, showing that your file is being saved.

5 The last step is to exit from the Editor and go back to the command prompt. You'll find the option to exit the program within the *File* menu that you've just used to save the file. To exit, press Alt-F again, then use the Down direction key to move the highlight down to the *Exit* command. Press Enter.

Error Message?
If you see an error message that says "File already exists. Overwrite?" it means a file exists already with the name you have chosen. Press N for no so you don't overwrite the existing file, and choose another name for the new file.

You have now created and saved a text file using the MS-DOS Editor utility. The file, called POEM.TXT, is stored on your hard disk. You'll learn more about the MS-DOS Editor utility on pages 98 to 99.

69

How to View the File

You have now learned to create a file using the MS-DOS Editor. Now that the file is stored on disk, let's look at it again, this time without using the Editor.

To check that the file you've just created is in the root directory of your hard disk, use the DIR command after the command prompt to see the contents of the current directory.

Looking for a File

```
C:\>DIR /p
```

1 Type DIR at the command prompt. There might be a lot of files, so try adding the /p switch to display the directory one screenful at a time.

2 Press Enter. A list will appear on your screen. Carefully look through to check that POEM.TXT (the name of your sample file) is there.

```
C:\>DIR /p

 Volume in drive C is WIZARD_DISK
 Volume Serial Number is 1A85-744C
 Directory of C:\

DOS          <DIR>        11-17-92   1:43p
WINWORD      <DIR>        02-10-93  12:29p
OLD_DOS   1  <DIR>        04-05-93   2:18p
POEM      TXT        119  05-07-93   1:00p
WINDOWS      <DIR>        03-01-93   5:24p
CONFIG    SYS        233  04-05-93   2:34p
COMMAND   COM      52925  03-10-93   6:00a
AUTOEXEC  BAT        521  04-13-93  11:25a
        8 file(s)       53798 bytes
```

To view the contents of the file you've just created, you can use the MS-DOS command TYPE. You may remember first meeting this command in Chapter 3 (see page 62). Because POEM.TXT is an unformatted text file, MS-DOS should have no difficulty displaying it on your screen for you to read.

Checking File Contents

```
C:\>TYPE POEM.TXT
```

1 Type the words TYPE POEM.TXT after the command prompt.

```
C:\>TYPE POEM.TXT
I always eat peas with honey
I've done it all my life,
They do taste kind of funny,
But it keeps them on the knife
```

2 Press Enter, and the text you typed in earlier should be displayed.

The "File not found" Message

If the filename was mistyped, was not saved, was named something different, or has been deleted, you'll see an error message saying "File not found." If you haven't mistyped, use the DIR command to display the directory contents and check whether the file has been saved under a slightly different name.

```
C:\>TYPE POEN.TXT
File not found - POEN.TXT

C:\>
```

Want More?

You can use the MORE command to look at big text files one screen at a time. To use it, type MORE at the command prompt, then a space, the "less than" character (<), another space, the filename, and press Enter. After seeing each screen, press any key, and the next screenful of material will appear. Try using the MORE command to view a file called README.TXT in the DOS directory. To do so, type MORE < \DOS\README.TXT and press Enter.

How to Print the File

You've seen how to display a file on the screen, but sometimes it is also useful to have a paper copy of the file. To print a text file, use the PRINT command. You can use this command to send several files to the printer in sequence — PRINT will make sure that the files are printed in order.

Printing a File

```
C:\>PRINT POEM.TXT
```

1 Type PRINT POEM.TXT at the command prompt.

2 Press Enter, and MS-DOS will ask for "Name of list device [PRN]:." Just press Enter; MS-DOS will assume that you want to use the printer port it calls PRN. You'll be asked for the name of the printer port only the first time you enter the PRINT command during a work session.

```
C:\>PRINT POEM.TXT
Name of list device [PRN]:
```

3 MS-DOS will then tell you that your file is being printed.

```
C:\>PRINT POEM.TXT
Name of list device [PRN]:
Resident part of PRINT installed

    C:\POEM.TXT is currently being printed
```

Print Plain!
PRINT will work only with files that contain plain, unformatted text. Many word processors add special formatting that the PRINT command won't print. Don't try to print these application files from the command prompt.

File Not Printing?
If the file is not printing, check that you have connected your printer to the PC, switched it on, and pressed the "online" button. Also, be sure that there is paper in the tray.

How to Rename the File

Sometimes you might want to change a file's name. MS-DOS will let you change any filename as long as the new name doesn't duplicate any that already exist in the same directory.

To rename a file, you need to use an MS-DOS command called REN (short for rename). When you enter the command REN, follow it on the same line with a space, the old name, a space, and then the new name. Try changing the name of the file POEM.TXT to a new name, SONG.TXT.

Changing a Filename

1 At the command prompt, type REN POEM.TXT SONG.TXT. Press Enter.

```
C:\>REN POEM.TXT SONG.TXT
```

2 Check that the change has taken place by typing the DIR command and pressing Enter. POEM.TXT will no longer be listed — but SONG.TXT should now appear in the list.

```
C:\>DIR
 Volume in drive C is WIZARD_DISK
 Volume Serial Number is 1A85-744C
 Directory of C:\

DOS          <DIR>       11-17-92    1:43p
WINWORD      <DIR>       02-10-93   12:29p
OLD_DOS  1   <DIR>       04-05-93    2:18p
SONG     TXT        119  05-07-93    1:00p
WINDOWS      <DIR>       03-01-93    5:24p
CONFIG   SYS        233  04-05-93    2:34p
COMMAND  COM      52925  03-10-93    6:00a
AUTOEXEC BAT        521  04-13-93   11:25a
         8 file(s)        53798 bytes
```

71

How to Copy the File

Check That Name!
MS-DOS does not check existing names before it copies a file. If you already have a file with the new name, it will be overwritten without notice. You can use the DIR command to check that there is not an existing file you are about to overwrite when you use the COPY command.

You can use the COPY command to make an exact duplicate of any file. When you copy a file, you need to name the new file. You can copy a file to a different directory or disk using the same name — or you can create a duplicate of a file in the same directory using a different filename. No two files in a directory can have the same names.

To create a second, identical file to SONG.TXT (which was called POEM.TXT before we renamed it), you can use this COPY command. Try creating a duplicate of SONG.TXT, called RHYME.TXT, within the same directory.

Making a Copy

1 At the command prompt, type COPY, a space, the name of the file you want to copy (SONG.TXT), a space, and the name of the new file that will hold the copy (RHYME.TXT).

```
C:\>COPY SONG.TXT RHYME.TXT
```

2 Press Enter. If your copying has been successful, MS-DOS will display the message "1 file(s) copied." If the copying wasn't successful, you are likely to see "File not found" on the screen. Check that you have correctly typed in the name of the file you want to copy.

```
C:\>COPY SONG.TXT RHYME.TXT
        1 file(s) copied
C:\>
```

```
C:\>DIR

 Volume in drive C is WIZARD_DISK
 Volume Serial Number is 1A85-744C
 Directory of C:\

DOS          <DIR>       11-17-92    1:43p
WINWORD      <DIR>       02-10-93   12:29p
OLD_DOS   1  <DIR>       04-05-93    2:18p
SONG      TXT      119   05-07-93    1:00p
RHYME     TXT      119   05-07-93    1:00p
WINDOWS      <DIR>       03-01-93    5:24p
CONFIG    SYS      233   04-05-93    2:34p
COMMAND   COM    52925   03-10-93    6:00a
AUTOEXEC  BAT      521   04-13-93   11:25a
        9 file(s)        53917 bytes
                      65075200 bytes free

C:\>
```

3 If the file has been copied, use the DIR command to display the directory contents. You will see that both the SONG.TXT and RHYME.TXT files appear in the current directory.

Bulk Copying?
You can copy more than a single file at one time. Doing this involves the use of "wildcards," which replace a single character or group of characters in a filename (see page 86).

You'll find out how to copy or move a file to a different directory on your hard disk on pages 77 and 78 and how to copy a file to a floppy disk on page 84. You can also copy more than one file at a time — see page 86.

How to Delete a File

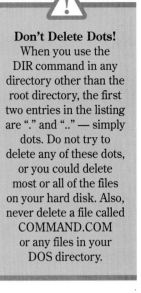

You've just made a second copy of SONG.TXT called RHYME.TXT. You don't need two files with the same contents, so how do you get rid of one? Use the DEL command to delete a file.

Removing a File from a Directory

```
C:\>DEL SONG.TXT
```

1 To delete your original file SONG.TXT, type DEL SONG.TXT at the command prompt and then press Enter.

```
C:\>DIR
```

2 Your file will be deleted, and you'll return to the command prompt. Now type in DIR and press Enter to display a list of files stored in the current directory.

```
C:\>DIR
 Volume in drive C is WIZARD_DISK
 Volume Serial Number is 1A85-744C
 Directory of C:\

DOS          <DIR>      11-17-92   1:43p
WINWORD       <DIR>     02-10-93  12:29p
OLD_DOS  1   <DIR>      04-05-93   2:18p
RHYME    TXT       119  05-07-93   1:00p
WINDOWS       <DIR>     03-01-93   5:24p
CONFIG   SYS       233  04-05-93   2:34p
COMMAND  COM     52925  03-10-93   6:00a
AUTOEXEC BAT       521  04-13-93  11:25a
         8 file(s)       53798 bytes
                      65048576 bytes free
```

3 Verify that SONG.TXT has been deleted from the directory.

How to Recover a File

Suppose you delete a file and wish immediately afterward that you hadn't? MS-DOS includes a special command that will restore a file. That may sound too good to be true, but it works. You must remember one important rule — retrieve your file as soon as possible.

Retrieving a Deleted File

```
C:\>UNDELETE
```

1 Try to restore the SONG.TXT file that you have just deleted by typing UNDELETE at the command prompt and pressing Enter.

2 MS-DOS will look for recoverable files that have been deleted recently and will ask if you want to undelete each one. Type Y for yes when asked about SONG.TXT and press Enter.

```
Directory:
File Specifications: *.*

        Delete Sentry control file not found.

        Deletion-tracking file not found.

        MS-DOS directory contains   1 deleted files.
        Of those,   1 files may be recovered.

Using the MS-DOS directory method.

        ?ONG    TXT    119  05-07-93 1.00p  ...A  Undelete<Y/N>?
```

Quick Retreat
If you accidentally delete a file, stop what you are doing and try to undelete the file using the UNDELETE command immediately. For more information about the Undelete utility, see page 110.

3 MS-DOS will then ask you to enter the first character of the name of the file you want to recover. In this instance, type S, and your file will be restored.

```
        ?ONG    TXT    119  05-07-93 1.00p  ...A  Undelete<Y/N>?Y
        Please type the first character for ?ONG    .TXT: S
File successfully undeleted.
```

Dabbling With Directories

S O FAR, YOU'VE LEARNED HOW to create a file, rename it, copy it, and delete it. As explained already, files are organized on a disk in individual work areas called directories. The main, or root, directory can contain files and other directories. Look at the diagram on page 57 to remind yourself of how storing files on disk is like storing documents in a filing cabinet. Keeping this familiar image in mind will help you when you are using MS-DOS to create and navigate around directories.

In Chapter 3, you learned how to use the DIR command to display lists of all the files and subdirectories within any directory on a disk. But suppose you are interested only in the directories, and not the files, on your disk? The answer is to modify the DIR command to list only the subdirectories in your current directory.

> **No Luck with the /ad Switch?**
> If you are using an older version of MS-DOS, the /ad switch might not work. An alternative is to type in DIR and then *. (that's an asterisk followed by a period) and press Enter.

`C:\>DIR /ad`

Listing Subdirectories

First make sure you are working in the root directory of your hard disk by typing in CD, a space, and a backslash at the command prompt and pressing Enter.

1 Now type DIR at the command prompt, but this time add a switch, /ad, at the end of the command before pressing Enter.

2 You'll now see a listing of only the subdirectories of your root directory.

```
C:\>DIR /ad

 Volume in drive C is WIZARD_DISK
 Volume Serial Number is 1A85-744C
 Directory of C:\

DOS            <DIR>      11-17-92    1:43p
WINWORD        <DIR>      02-10-93   12:29p
OLD_DOS   1    <DIR>      04-05-93    2:18p
WINDOWS        <DIR>      03-01-93    5:24p
        4 file(s)                   0 bytes
                          64987136 bytes free

C:\>
```

VIEWING THE WHOLE DIRECTORY TREE

You cannot use the DIR command to see a listing of directories more than one level below the current directory unless you first move down the directory tree structure. However, MS-DOS has another command, called TREE, that will give a visual display of all the directories and subdirectories that branch off from any specified directory. Viewing this type of display can help when you're trying to find a subdirectory.

`C:\>TREE`

1 To see the whole directory tree structure below the root directory, type TREE at the command prompt.

2 Press Enter. MS-DOS spends a few seconds looking for all the directories on the disk; it then displays a directory structure. You may discover you have far more directories on your disk than you thought!

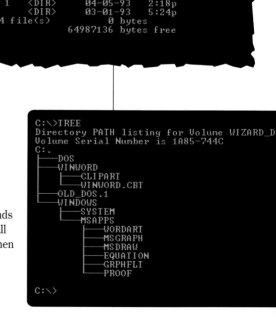

```
C:\>TREE
Directory PATH listing for Volume WIZARD_D
Volume Serial Number is 1A85-744C
C:.
├──DOS
├──WINWORD
│   ├──CLIPART
│   └──WINWORD.CBT
├──OLD_DOS.1
└──WINDOWS
    ├──SYSTEM
    └──MSAPPS
        ├──WORDART
        ├──MSGRAPH
        ├──MSDRAW
        ├──EQUATION
        ├──GRPHFLT
        └──PROOF

C:\>
```

How to Move Around the Directory Tree

You use the CD command to move from one directory to another. To do so, you type CD at the command prompt, followed by a space and the full pathname of the directory you want to move to.

MOVING DOWN TO THE DOS SUBDIRECTORY
Try using the CD command to move to the DOS subdirectory of your root directory. Once you've moved there, you can use the DIR command to see what is in the DOS directory.

```
C:\>CD \DOS
```

1 Type CD, a space, and then \DOS at the command prompt.

```
C:\>CD \DOS
C:\DOS>
```

2 Press Enter. The prompt will change to C:\DOS>, thus indicating that you are now located in the DOS subdirectory.

MOVING UP THE TREE STRUCTURE
As previously explained, to move to the top of the tree structure — the root directory — you just type in CD, a space, a backslash, and then press Enter.

Another method of reverting to the root directory from the DOS directory is to issue a CD .. command. This command moves you just one level at a time up the tree structure — that is, from a subdirectory to its parent directory.

```
C:\DOS>CD ..
```

1 Type CD .. at the command prompt. Include a space between CD and the two periods.

```
C:\DOS>CD ..
C:\>
```

2 Press Enter and you'll be returned to the root directory.

Need a Backslash?
When using the CD command to move down the directory tree, you can omit the first backslash in the full pathname of the directory you are moving to. For example, the command CD WINDOWS would move you straight to the WINDOWS directory. If you do use the backslash, MS-DOS will move to the root directory then move down the path.

Know Your Place!
MS-DOS assumes that the commands you type apply to the contents of the current drive and directory. Be sure you know where you are all the time so you don't accidentally delete or mislocate files. You can always find out the directory you are in by typing CD at the command prompt and pressing Enter.

How to Create Directories

If you want to organize your hard disk by adding new directories to change the existing tree structure, the first step is to create one or more new directories. The MS-DOS command you use to create a directory is MD (short for make directory).

TWO NEW DIRECTORIES

Let's create two new directories, both located in the root directory. Again, before proceeding, make sure you are in the root directory of your hard disk by typing in CD \ and pressing Enter.

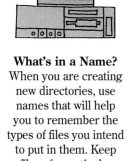

What's in a Name?
When you are creating new directories, use names that will help you to remember the types of files you intend to put in them. Keep files of a particular type, or files related to a particular project, in the same directory.

Keep it Short!
You can use a file extension with directories but more typing is needed. Try to avoid extensions when naming directories and keep your names to eight characters or less.

ROOT DIRECTORY

C:\

\DOS

\HOBBIES

\LETTERS

RHYME.TXT

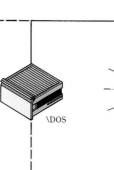

```
C:\>MD LETTERS

C:\>MD HOBBIES

C:\>
```

1 Create two new subdirectories of the root directory called LETTERS and HOBBIES by typing MD LETTERS and pressing Enter, and then typing MD HOBBIES and pressing Enter.

Keep it Simple!
You will find it easier to use directories if you stick to creating new directories in your root directory. Creating complicated tree structures in which directories hold many subdirectories may confuse your work.

2 Type DIR /ad and press Enter. You will see a list of all the subdirectories of the root directory, among which are your new subdirectories, LETTERS and HOBBIES.

```
C:\>DIR /ad

 Volume in drive C is WIZARD_DISK
 Volume Serial Number is 1A85-744C
 Directory of C:\

DOS          <DIR>      11-17-92   1:43p
WINWORD      <DIR>      02-10-93  12:29p
OLD_DOS   1  <DIR>      04-05-93   2:18p
WINDOWS      <DIR>      03-01-93   5:24p
LETTERS      <DIR>      05-07-93   5:01p
HOBBIES      <DIR>      05-07-93   5:01p
      6 file(s)              0 bytes
                    65079296 bytes free
```

How to Copy a File to a New Directory

Now that you've created some new directories, you've started to organize your hard disk. The next step is to learn how to copy files to the new directories. If you store all the files you create in the root directory, you would soon find it hard to locate files.

Earlier in this chapter, you created a file called POEM.TXT that you renamed SONG.TXT and then duplicated as a file called RHYME.TXT. The file RHYME.TXT is still in the root directory — let's copy it to the LETTERS directory you've created. To do this, you use the COPY command. When copying a file to a new directory, you specify first the full pathname of the file you want to copy, followed by the pathname of the directory to which you want to copy the file.

ROOT DIRECTORY

C:\

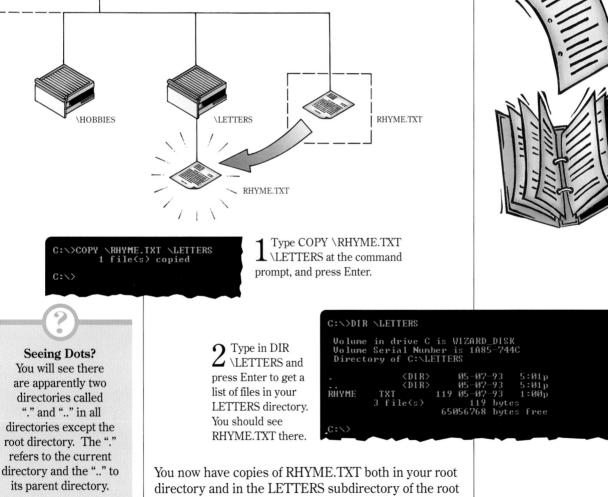

\HOBBIES

\LETTERS

RHYME.TXT

RHYME.TXT

```
C:\>COPY \RHYME.TXT \LETTERS
        1 file(s) copied

C:\>
```

1 Type COPY \RHYME.TXT \LETTERS at the command prompt, and press Enter.

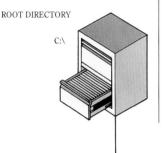

Seeing Dots?
You will see there are apparently two directories called "." and ".." in all directories except the root directory. The "." refers to the current directory and the ".." to its parent directory.

2 Type in DIR \LETTERS and press Enter to get a list of files in your LETTERS directory. You should see RHYME.TXT there.

```
C:\>DIR \LETTERS

 Volume in drive C is WIZARD_DISK
 Volume Serial Number is 1A85-744C
 Directory of C:\LETTERS

.            <DIR>      05-07-93   5:01p
..           <DIR>      05-07-93   5:01p
RHYME    TXT      119   05-07-93   1:00p
        3 file(s)        119 bytes
                    65056768 bytes free

C:\>
```

You now have copies of RHYME.TXT both in your root directory and in the LETTERS subdirectory of the root directory on your hard disk.

How to Move a File to a New Directory

Moving a file is different from copying a file in that no duplicate of the file is left in the original, or source, directory. In previous versions of MS-DOS, to move a file you first had to copy it to the new directory using the COPY command and then delete it from the old directory using the DEL command. But with MS-DOS 6 you can use a new command, MOVE, to transfer a file from one directory to another. After MOVE, you type in first the pathname of the file you want to move and then the pathname of the directory you want to move it to. Let's use the MOVE command to move RHYME.TXT from your LETTERS directory to the HOBBIES directory.

Need Help?
Don't forget that online help is available with all MS-DOS commands. For example, for more information about the MOVE command, type HELP MOVE at the command prompt and press Enter.

Any Old Files?
When reorganizing files, you might find it convenient to create a special directory called OLD. You can then move into it any old files you suspect you no longer need but don't want to delete just yet.

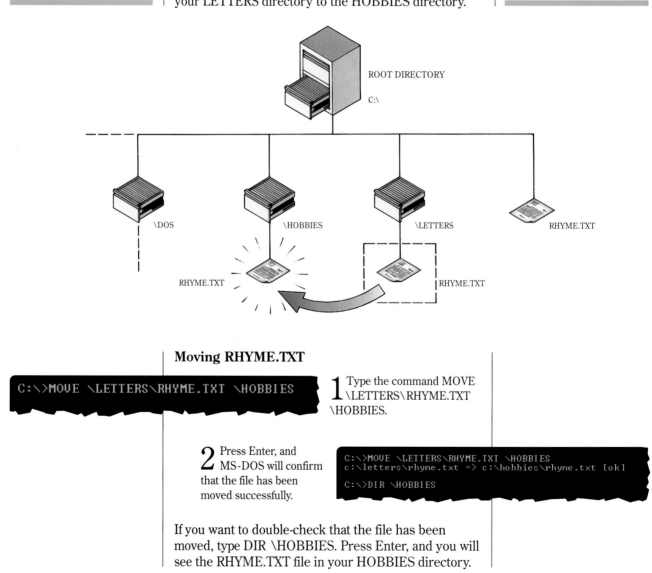

ROOT DIRECTORY
C:\

\DOS   \HOBBIES   \LETTERS   RHYME.TXT

RHYME.TXT   RHYME.TXT

Moving RHYME.TXT

```
C:\>MOVE \LETTERS\RHYME.TXT \HOBBIES
```

1 Type the command MOVE \LETTERS\RHYME.TXT \HOBBIES.

2 Press Enter, and MS-DOS will confirm that the file has been moved successfully.

```
C:\>MOVE \LETTERS\RHYME.TXT \HOBBIES
c:\letters\rhyme.txt => c:\hobbies\rhyme.txt [ok]

C:\>DIR \HOBBIES
```

If you want to double-check that the file has been moved, type DIR \HOBBIES. Press Enter, and you will see the RHYME.TXT file in your HOBBIES directory.

MOVE AND CHANGE

When using the MOVE command to move a single file, you can rename the file as you are moving it. To do this, you use the MOVE command as normal, but at the end of the command line you add the new name of the file after the pathname of the directory you are moving it to. Let's move the copy of RHYME.TXT, which is still in your root directory, to your LETTERS directory and at the same time rename it PEAS.TXT.

1 Type MOVE \RHYME.TXT \LETTERS\PEAS.TXT.

```
C:\>MOUE \RHYME.TXT \LETTERS\PEAS.TXT
```

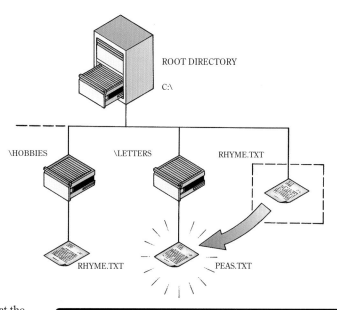

2 Press Enter, and MS-DOS will confirm that the move has been completed successfully. Now type in DIR \LETTERS and press Enter to check that a file called PEAS.TXT is now in the LETTERS directory.

How to Rename a Directory

In addition to its uses in moving and renaming files, you can also use the MOVE command to rename a directory. To do this, after the MOVE command you type in first the pathname of the directory you want to rename, then a space, a backslash, and its new name. Let's rename your LETTERS directory REPORTS.

```
C:\>MOUE \RHYME.TXT \LETTERS\PEAS.TXT
c:\rhyme.txt => c:\letters\peas.txt [ok]

C:\>DIR \LETTERS

 Volume in drive C is WIZARD_DISK
 Volume Serial Number is 1A85-744C
 Directory of C:\LETTERS

.            <DIR>       05-07-93    5:01p
..           <DIR>       05-07-93    5:01p
PEAS     TXT      119    05-07-93    1:00p
        3 file(s)            119 bytes
                      65019904 bytes free

C:\>
```

1 Type MOVE \LETTERS \REPORTS and press Enter. MS-DOS will confirm that the directory has been renamed.

```
C:\>MOUE \LETTERS \REPORTS
c:\letters => c:\reports [ok]
```

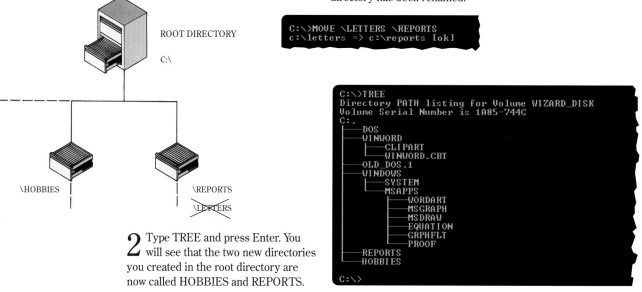

2 Type TREE and press Enter. You will see that the two new directories you created in the root directory are now called HOBBIES and REPORTS.

```
C:\>TREE
Directory PATH listing for Volume WIZARD_DISK
Volume Serial Number is 1A85-744C
C:.
├───DOS
├───WINWORD
│   ├───CLIPART
│   └───WINWORD.CBT
├───OLD_DOS.1
├───WINDOWS
│   ├───SYSTEM
│   └───MSAPPS
│       ├───WORDART
│       ├───MSGRAPH
│       ├───MSDRAW
│       ├───EQUATION
│       ├───GRPHFLT
│       └───PROOF
├───REPORTS
└───HOBBIES

C:\>
```

How to Delete a Directory

If you need to reorganize your disk structure, you might find you want to delete a directory. You can delete a directory by using the command RD (short for remove directory). However, before you can delete a directory using this command, you must first delete all the files (and any subdirectories) in it. MS-DOS 6 features a new command, DELTREE, that allows you to delete a directory and its entire contents in one step. Let's use DELTREE to delete the REPORTS directory; at the same time you will delete the only file contained within it (PEAS.TXT).

Care with DELTREE!
You should use the DELTREE command with care. Make sure that you do not need any of the files (or subdirectories) within the directory you are about to delete before you use DELTREE.

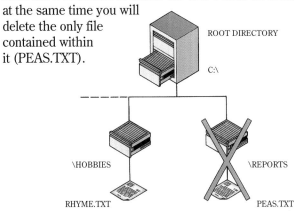

ROOT DIRECTORY

C:\

\HOBBIES   \REPORTS

RHYME.TXT   PEAS.TXT

Removing a Directory
You cannot use the RD command to remove the directory you are currently in. You must first move up the directory tree, then type RD, a space, and the pathname of the directory you want to remove. In contrast, if you use DELTREE to try to delete your current directory, you will not remove it, but you will empty it of its entire contents.

Using the DELTREE Command

```
C:\>DELTREE \REPORTS
```

1 Type DELTREE \REPORTS. (Be careful when you do this — only use DELTREE on a directory you want to delete for good.)

2 Press Enter. MS-DOS will ask you to confirm that you want to delete the REPORTS directory. Type Y and press Enter. MS-DOS will confirm that it is deleting the directory.

```
C:\>DELTREE \REPORTS
Delete directory "\reports" and all its subdirectories? [yn] y
Deleting \reports...

C:\>
```

3 Now type TREE and press Enter. The full tree structure that exists below your root directory will be displayed, and you will see that the REPORTS directory has disappeared.

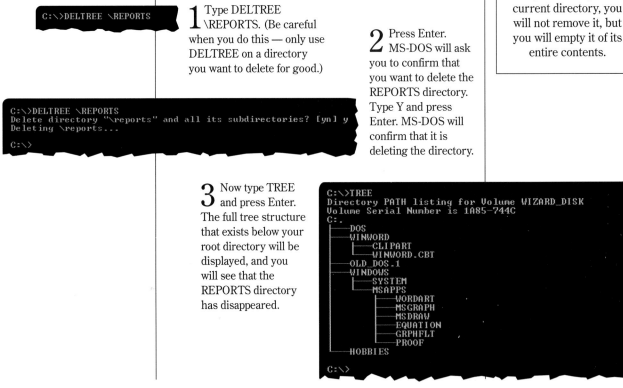

```
C:\>TREE
Directory PATH listing for Volume WIZARD_DISK
Volume Serial Number is 1A85-744C
C:.
├───DOS
├───WINWORD
│   ├───CLIPART
│   └───WINWORD.CBT
├───OLD_DOS.1
├───WINDOWS
│   ├───SYSTEM
│   └───MSAPPS
│       ├───WORDART
│       ├───MSGRAPH
│       ├───MSDRAW
│       ├───EQUATION
│       ├───GRPHFLT
│       └───PROOF
└───HOBBIES

C:\>
```

How to Find a Lost File

If you are not sure in what directory you put a file and can't find it by checking directory listings, you can let MS-DOS find it for you. At the command prompt, you type in the DIR command, a space, a backslash, and then the name of the file you are looking for, another space, and then the /s switch. When you press Enter, MS-DOS will search through your disk looking for the directory that contains the file. If MS-DOS finds the lost file, it will tell you the name of the directory it is in and some details about the file.

Lost a Directory?
If you have lost a whole directory, try moving to the root directory and then using the TREE command to display the full tree structure. Use the Pause key as the directory tree scrolls by if it is large. Examine the tree carefully to see if you can find your lost directory.

Network Care!
If your PC is connected to a network, you might find that the system administrator has some rules to help manage all the PCs. Check with that person before you become too energetic with creating and deleting directories and files.

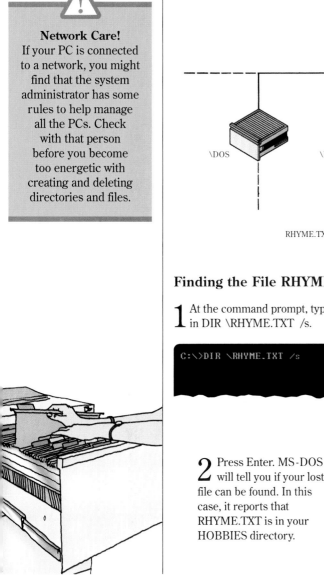

ROOT DIRECTORY

C:\

\DOS

\HOBBIES

RHYME.TXT

Finding the File RHYME. TXT

1 At the command prompt, type in DIR \RHYME.TXT /s.

```
C:\>DIR \RHYME.TXT /s
```

2 Press Enter. MS-DOS will tell you if your lost file can be found. In this case, it reports that RHYME.TXT is in your HOBBIES directory.

```
C:\>DIR \RHYME.TXT /s

 Volume in drive C is WIZARD_DISK
 Volume Serial Number is 1A85-744C

Directory of C:\HOBBIES

RHYME    TXT       119 05-07-93   1:00p
        1 file(s)          119 bytes

Total files listed:
        1 file(s)          119 bytes
                      64940032 bytes free

C:\>
```

Disky Business

Y OU WILL FIND IT MOST CONVENIENT TO WORK mainly from your PC's hard disk, but you'll need to use floppy disks for making backup copies of files and for transferring information between machines. Before you can use a new floppy disk, you must first format it.

Formatting a Floppy Disk

Formatting a disk involves preparing it so that it is organized in a way MS-DOS can recognize and use. MS-DOS formats a disk so that it can find and retrieve files (see page 26). Floppy disks of either size can store different amounts of data depending on their capacity, which can be either low or high. Floppy disk drives also have different capacities. Some older PCs have low-capacity drives, whereas most newer PCs have high-capacity drives.

Unless you indicate otherwise, MS-DOS will format a new floppy disk to the maximum capacity of the drive you format it in; if you format a low-capacity floppy disk in a high-capacity drive, you must tell MS-DOS to format the disk to low capacity.

High or Low?

Determine if the floppy disk you want to format is low- or high-capacity by checking the label (see "Floppy Disk Capacities," opposite, and the information on pages 24 and 25).

Capacities and Drives

Before you format a floppy disk you should first know its capacity. You should also know whether the floppy disk drive(s) on your PC are high- or low-capacity: check your PC's documentation and refer to "Floppy Disk Drive Capacities," opposite. Your PC may well have two floppy disk drives, in which case you should also determine which is A and which is B (see page 62).

Note that if you have only one floppy disk drive it is always named drive A.

Don't Mix High and Low!
Avoid formatting a high-capacity disk in a low-capacity drive. It is a waste of a more expensive disk, and a high-capacity disk formatted to low-capacity may not be readable by some machines. Similarly, avoid formatting a low-capacity disk to high-capacity because errors are likely.

Drive Carefully
To format a disk, you must insert it into the correct drive on the front of your system unit, noting whether the drive is drive A or B.

HOW TO FORMAT A NEW DISK

Steps to Formatting

Insert the floppy disk into the correct disk drive, noting whether you are using disk drive A or B. The following steps assume that you are using disk drive A; if you are using drive B, simply substitute B in the instructions.

```
C:\>FORMAT A:
```

1 Type the command FORMAT A: directly after the command prompt.

```
C:\>FORMAT A: /f:720
```

2 If you are formatting a low-capacity disk in a high-capacity drive, add a switch to the FORMAT command. This switch is /f:720 for a 3½-inch disk and /f:360 for a 5¼-inch disk. In all other cases, you do not need to use a switch. (You should not try to format a high-capacity disk in a low-capacity drive.)

```
C:\>FORMAT A:
Insert new diskette for drive A:
and press ENTER when ready...

Checking existing disk format.
Formatting 1.44M
_4 percent completed.
```

3 Press Enter. You will be asked to insert the new disk in drive A. Press Enter again and you will see a message on the screen telling you the capacity to which the disk is being formatted.

```
Volume label (11 characters, ENTER for none)?
```

4 Once formatting is finished, MS-DOS asks if you want to give the disk a volume label. If you want, you can type in a name for the entire disk. Otherwise, just press Enter. Whether or not you add a label, you can now use the floppy disk to store files.

HOW TO UNDO FORMATTING

Formatting a new disk prepares it for use by MS-DOS; formatting an already used floppy disk or a hard disk will erase its contents. If you accidentally format a disk and lose the files on it, you can undo the formatting action by using the MS-DOS command UNFORMAT. The command will return either a hard or floppy disk to the way it was before you formatted it. To rescue data, enter UNFORMAT followed by the name of the disk you accidentally formatted. For example, you can enter the command UNFORMAT A: to restore your floppy disk to its previous condition.

Floppy Disk Drive Capacities

Disk-Drive Type	Capacity
3½-inch low-capacity drive	720KB
3½-inch high-capacity drive	1.44MB
5¼-inch low-capacity drive	360KB
5¼-inch high-capacity drive	1.2MB

Floppy Disk Capacities

Disk Type	Capacity	Identification on Box or Label
3½-inch low-capacity floppy disk	720KB	DS/DD (double-sided, double-density) or 2DD
3½-inch high-capacity floppy disk	1.44MB	DS/HD (double-sided, high-density) or 2HD
5¼-inch low-capacity floppy disk	360KB	DS/DD (double-sided, double-density) or 2DD
5¼-inch high-capacity floppy disk	1.2MB	DS/HD (double-sided, high-density) or 2HD

Copying to a Floppy Disk

Most of the time, you'll be saving files on your hard disk. A hard disk can store much more information than a floppy disk and processes information faster. However, you'll need to copy files onto floppy disks when you make backup copies of hard disk files or when you want to transfer information to another computer. Keep in mind that you can use any of the MS-DOS directory commands with a floppy disk.

Full Up!
If you see the MS-DOS message "Insufficient disk space" when you try to copy files to a floppy disk, it simply means the disk is full. When this message appears, either delete some files you no longer need or use another floppy disk.

Making a Floppy Copy

```
C:\>COPY \HOBBIES\RHYME.TXT A:
```

1 To copy a file from the hard disk to a floppy disk, you type the COPY command followed by the full pathname of the file you want to copy, and then the name of the floppy disk drive containing the disk you want to use. For example, to copy the file RHYME.TXT from your HOBBIES directory on drive C to a floppy disk in drive A, type the command COPY \HOBBIES\RHYME.TXT A: after the command prompt.

```
Directory of A:\

FLUFFY     BMP     287925  11-20-91   12:00
BRYN1      DOC        102  03-08-93    7:48
BRYN2      DOC       5115  05-06-93    6:32
LETTER1    DOC       6766  03-10-92    3:10
CHART3     XLS        500  04-05-93    2:12
ARTICLE1   TXT       4717  05-04-93    4:34
RHYME      TXT        119  05-07-93    1:00
           7 file(s)            305244 bytes
                               906752 bytes fre
```

2 After you've copied a file onto a floppy disk, use the command DIR A: to check that the file appears on the list of contents for the disk in drive A.

Duplicating Floppy Disks

Software for your PC is supplied on floppy disks. It is wise to duplicate these disks right away in case you make a mistake installing the software or in case you lose or damage the original disks.

Although it is useful for individual files, the COPY command cannot always be relied upon to create an accurate copy of a whole disk. Duplicating all the files on a floppy disk one file at a time could take a long time and you would find it annoying to type in the COPY command for each file. Furthermore, if the disk contains subdirectories, you would also have to re-create each subdirectory on the new disk.

To duplicate the contents of a floppy disk it is best to use the DISKCOPY command. This command duplicates everything, including all files and directory structures, from one disk to another.

Source and Target
When duplicating disks, MS-DOS refers to the original disk as the "source," whereas the disk you are copying to is called the "target." Be certain that they are clearly distinguishable before you start any duplicating.

SHORTCUT TO COPYING

The DISKCOPY command works only for duplicating the entire contents of one floppy disk onto another floppy disk of the same size and capacity. Note that it is not possible to use the DISKCOPY command to duplicate the contents of your hard disk.

If your PC has only one floppy disk drive, the DISK-COPY command will still work because it temporarily stores the files to be copied in memory and then asks you to swap disks before writing the files to the new floppy disk. If you have only one floppy disk drive on your PC, or if your two drives are different sizes, follow these steps:

From One Floppy Disk to Another

```
C:\>DISKCOPY A: A:
```

1 First type the command DISKCOPY A: A: and then press Enter.

```
C:\>DISKCOPY A: A:

Insert SOURCE diskette in drive A:

Press any key to continue . . . .
```

2 You will be asked to insert the disk to be copied (the source disk) into drive A and press any key.

Be Patient!
Take care when duplicating a set of disks to copy them one at a time. MS-DOS has finished duplicating a disk when it displays the message "Copy another diskette (Y/N)?"

3 After a few seconds, your PC will ask you to insert the second (target) disk. Take out the source, put in the target, and press any key. You may be asked to swap the disks several times.

```
C:\>DISKCOPY A: A:

Insert SOURCE diskette in drive A:

Press any key to continue . . .

Copying 80 tracks
15 sectors per track, 2 side(s)

Insert TARGET diskette in drive A:

Press any key to continue . . .
```

```
Press any key to continue . . .
Insert SOURCE diskette in drive A:
Press any key to continue . . .
Insert TARGET diskette in drive A:
Press any key to continue . . .
Copy another diskette (Y/N)?
```

4 When copying is completed, your PC asks if you want to copy another disk. Press Y for yes, or press N for no if you want to return to the command prompt.

Using Both Drives
If both floppy disk drives are the same size, use the command below to copy from a disk in drive A.

```
C:\>DISKCOPY A: B:
```

You can use DISKCOPY to copy from one floppy disk drive to another, but only if the two floppy disk drives are the same size. This method saves swapping disks back and forth — your source disk goes in one drive and the target disk goes in the other. For example, you can use the command DISKCOPY A: B: if you are copying from a disk in drive A to a disk in drive B.

First Write-Protect!
Before you duplicate a disk, it's a good idea to first write-protect it (see page 27). By doing this, you prevent any chance of the data on the source disk being overwritten during the duplicating procedure.

85

Wildcards

A LL THE COMMANDS FOR MANAGING FILES that you have used so far have applied to single files. You copied one file from one directory to another, renamed a file, and deleted a file. Using only the commands that you've learned about so far, copying all files from one directory into another would involve copying every file individually.

Fortunately, MS-DOS allows you to be much less specific, which can save you time and effort. Instead of copying one file at a time, you can ask MS-DOS to copy all the files in a directory or all the files with a particular extension, such as DOC.

Two Helpful "Jokers"

The two wildcard characters (*) and (?) work somewhat like jokers in a deck of cards. The asterisk (*) can represent any filename, extension, or both.

For example, *.* means all files. The question mark (?) is much less sweeping; it can stand for any single character in a filename, an extension, or both. You can use more than one question mark, each one representing a single character.

WILDCARDS FOR COPYING
If you want to copy a group of files, you need to specify all their filenames. Using wildcards simplifies the process. All you have to do is identify the common elements in the group of filenames or their extensions, and use wildcards for the variable elements.

Copying All Files

```
C:\>COPY *.* \HOBBIES
```

1 To copy all the files in the root directory of your hard disk into your HOBBIES directory, type COPY *.* \HOBBIES at the command prompt.

```
C:\>COPY *.* \HOBBIES
SONG.TXT
CONFIG.SYS
COMMAND.COM
AUTOEXEC.BAT
    4 file(s) copied
```

2 Press Enter, and the files will be copied into the HOBBIES directory. MS-DOS lists them as they are copied.

What Use Is "?" ?
You will find the ? wildcard useful for groups of files whose names vary in just one or two characters. For example, if you have a group of 500 files called TOM1.DOC through TOM500.DOC, you can identify them all with TOM???.DOC.

Longer Alternative

```
C:\>COPY ????????.??? \HOBBIES
```

You could have used the ? wildcard, but that would have required eleven question marks. The ? wildcard matches any single character — so eight question marks, a period, and three more question marks represents any filename.

Copying Similar Files

1 To copy all the files with a TXT extension from your DOS directory into your HOBBIES directory, type COPY \DOS*.TXT \HOBBIES and press Enter.

```
C:\>COPY \DOS\*.TXT \HOBBIES
```

```
C:\>DIR \HOBBIES

 Volume in drive C is WIZARD_DISK
 Volume Serial Number is 1A85-744C
 Directory of C:\HOBBIES

.             <DIR>      05-07-93    5:01p
..            <DIR>      05-07-93    5:01p
RHYME    TXT      119    05-07-93    1:00p
SONG     TXT      119    05-07-93    1:00p
CONFIG   SYS      233    04-05-93    2:34p
COMMAND  COM    52925    03-10-93    6:00a
AUTOEXEC BAT      521    04-13-93   11:25a
NETWORKS TXT    23444    03-10-93    6:00a
OS2      TXT     6358    03-10-93    6:00a
README   TXT    61857    03-10-93    6:00a
        10 file(s)        145576 bytes
                        64821248 bytes free
```

2 Now use the command DIR \HOBBIES to view a listing of all the files in your HOBBIES directory. You will see that there are now some more files with the TXT extension in this directory.

Practice using the wildcard characters by copying the files named DOSSHELL (but with varied extensions) contained in the DOS directory to your HOBBIES directory. To do this, type COPY \DOS\DOSSHELL.* \HOBBIES. This command copies several files. You can then use the DIR \HOBBIES command to see the files listed in your HOBBIES directory.

RENAMING AND DELETING
Note that using wildcards is not limited to just the COPY command. You can also use wildcards to move files using the MOVE command, delete a group of files using the DEL command, or even rename a whole group of files using REN.

How to Rename and Delete Files

```
C:\>REN \HOBBIES\*.TXT *.ASC
```

1 To change the name of all files in the HOBBIES directory with a TXT extension to an ASC extension, type REN \HOBBIES*.TXT *.ASC. Press Enter, use the DIR \HOBBIES command, and you will see that all the files that had a TXT extension now appear with an ASC extension.

```
C:\>DEL \HOBBIES\*.ASC
```

2 To delete all files with the ASC extension from your HOBBIES directory, type DEL \HOBBIES*.ASC at the command prompt. Press Enter and all files that end with the extension ASC will be removed from the directory.

Care When Deleting!
Be careful when using the DEL command and wildcards. Using the command DEL *.* will delete all the files in your current directory. Always check which directory you are in and be sure you want to delete all files in it before you use the DEL *.* command. You can type DIR *.* to see what DEL *.* will delete.

Simpler Still
You can use *. (an asterisk and a period) to match only filenames that do not have an extension (directories, typically). To match all filenames starting with the same letter, you use only the asterisk in combination with the letter. For example, use M* to match all filenames starting with M.

Two Special Files

WHEN YOU SWITCH ON YOUR PC, MS-DOS is automatically loaded from your hard disk into your PC's memory. Two special files that are loaded from the root directory during this process — CONFIG.SYS and AUTOEXEC.BAT — are used by MS-DOS to configure and set up the PC. Knowing what they contain helps you to control MS-DOS and modify the way it works.

CONFIG.SYS and AUTOEXEC.BAT are both text files, so you can use the TYPE command to see what is inside them and you can use the Editor to modify them. Let's take a look at each of the files to see what they contain.

The CONFIG.SYS File

The CONFIG.SYS file controls your PC's configuration by setting up the memory and other system components. When you install a new application or add a new piece of hardware, you are sometimes asked to modify this file afterward. When you make changes to your CONFIG.SYS file, they take effect the next time you start your computer.

```
C:\>TYPE C:\CONFIG.SYS
```

1 Type TYPE C:\CONFIG.SYS at the command prompt and press Enter to view the contents of your CONFIG.SYS file.

```
C:\>TYPE C:\CONFIG.SYS
DEVICE=C:\DOS\SETVER.EXE
DEVICE=C:\DOS\HIMEM.SYS
DOS=HIGH,UMB
FILES=40
BUFFERS=30
STACKS=9,256
SHELL=C:\DOS\COMMAND.COM C:\DOS\ /p

C:\>
```

2 Your CONFIG.SYS file might have a few less or a few more lines than the one shown here, but it will be similar in structure.

WHAT THE LINES MEAN

Each line in the CONFIG.SYS file includes a command that controls a certain aspect of your machine. The first line — DEVICE=C:\DOS\SETVER.EXE — in the example shown here is a small utility file in your DOS subdirectory that supports programs written for previous versions of MS-DOS.

The second and third lines configure the memory in your PC so that applications that run on MS-DOS will operate as efficiently as possible. (See page 118 in the Reference Section for advice on how to configure your memory to run more efficiently.)

The fourth line — FILES=40 — informs MS-DOS how many files it can open at any one time, and the BUFFERS and STACKS lines tell MS-DOS how much memory to reserve for transferring information to and from your disks.

The last line tells MS-DOS where to find its own main program file, COMMAND.COM. In our example, the file is in the DOS directory, although it is typically also found in the root directory. COMMAND.COM checks the commands you type in at the command prompt and acts on them accordingly.

The AUTOEXEC.BAT File

The other important MS-DOS file stored in your root directory is the AUTOEXEC.BAT file. This is a *batch file* — a special file that contains MS-DOS commands to be executed one after the other (see page 119 in the Reference Section for more on batch files). MS-DOS automatically carries out all the commands stored in this file when you first switch on your PC. Once you have developed some expertise, you can modify your AUTOEXEC.BAT file so that certain instructions — like running a favorite application — will be carried out automatically when you start your machine.

What's in Your AUTOEXEC.BAT File?

1 Type TYPE C:\AUTOEXEC.BAT at the command prompt.

```
C:\>TYPE C:\AUTOEXEC.BAT
```

```
C:\>TYPE C:\AUTOEXEC.BAT
@ECHO OFF
PROMPT $p$g
PATH C:\DOS;C:\WINDOWS
SET TEMP=C:\DOS

C:\>
```

2 Press Enter, and the contents of your AUTOEXEC.BAT file will appear on screen.

Change with Caution
Making changes to your AUTOEXEC.BAT or CONFIG.SYS files affects the way your PC performs. Before modifying these files in any way, make backup copies; if the changes you make don't work as you expect them to, you can then restore the original files.

Once again, the lines displayed on your screen might be a little different than those shown above.

@ECHO OFF instructs MS-DOS not to display commands as they are carried out in batch files; this minimizes the amount of information you see when your computer boots up. The PROMPT line determines the appearance of the command prompt — in this example it indicates "C:\>." The PATH line tells MS-DOS where to look on your hard disk for programs. In the above example, MS-DOS is told to look in the DOS directory and then the WINDOWS directory if it cannot find a file in the current directory.

HOW TO EDIT THE FILES

You sometimes need to modify the instructions in your CONFIG.SYS or AUTOEXEC.BAT files when you buy a new piece of hardware or add an application to your hard disk. This can be done with the MS-DOS Editor; see page 98 for instructions on using this program.

Take Care!
If you modify your AUTOEXEC.BAT or CONFIG.SYS file and then encounter problems when you restart your PC, check that the alterations you made were correct. You may have typed in something incorrectly.

5

MS-DOS Utilities

*If you're finding it difficult to remember
MS-DOS commands, you should find this chapter
useful because it shows you how to choose commands
from a menu with the aid of the MS-DOS Shell. You'll
also learn more about the MS-DOS Editor and its simple
word processing facilities. And you'll find out how you
can use some new features in MS-DOS version 6, such
as the defragmentation and Anti-Virus utilities, to
keep your computer in tip-top condition.*

THE MS-DOS SHELL
THE MS-DOS EDITOR • BACKUP AND RESTORE
DOUBLESPACE • ANTI-VIRUS UTILITY
DEFRAGMENTATION • UNDELETE

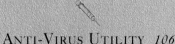

The MS-DOS Shell

U P UNTIL NOW, ALL THE COMMANDS you've learned have had to be typed in at the MS-DOS command line. If you're finding it hard to remember which commands do what, or the correct way to type them in, there's help around the corner in the form of the MS-DOS Shell. The MS-DOS Shell is a program stored in the DOS directory on your hard disk. It displays files, subdirectories, and menus of MS-DOS commands on the screen all at the same time, so carrying out an action, such as moving a file, is easy.

Instead of having to remember MS-DOS commands to type at the command prompt, you can select the commands from menus. If you have a mouse, using the MS-DOS Shell is simple; you can also use the Shell with a keyboard.

Starting the Shell

To start the Shell, type DOSSHELL at the command prompt and then press Enter. After a couple of seconds the program will appear in the form of a *window*.

Disk Drive Icons
Usually only drives A, B, and C are represented, but if you are connected to a network or have additional drives more drive icons might be shown.

Menu Bar
This lists five menu names: File, Options, View, Tree, *and* Help. *Hidden underneath these menu names are drop-down menus, which let you select and carry out MS-DOS commands without typing them in.*

Directory Tree Area
The root directory is at the top with subdirectories branching off from it. The root directory is highlighted (selected), which means its contents are being displayed in the file list area.

Program List Area
This shows you the programs you can launch directly from the Shell.

Program Title Bar
This bar tells you that you are in the MS-DOS Shell program.

File List Area
This shows the files stored in whichever directory is highlighted in the Directory Tree *area.*

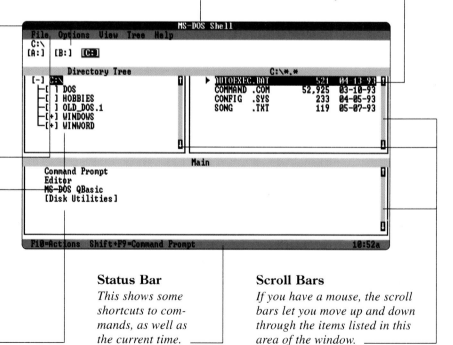

Status Bar
This shows some shortcuts to commands, as well as the current time.

Scroll Bars
If you have a mouse, the scroll bars let you move up and down through the items listed in this area of the window.

Getting Around the Shell

If you have a mouse installed on your PC, you will see a pointer (either a rectangular shape or an arrow) on your screen. You use the mouse to move the pointer around the screen and to select options. If you don't have a mouse, you can use certain keys to perform the same tasks. For now, there are three basic mouse skills that you'll need to master in order to use the MS-DOS Shell: pointing, clicking, and dragging.

Rectangular Pointer

Arrow Pointer

POINTING
Move the mouse slowly and watch how the pointer moves in unison. Use it to "point" at directory and file listings by positioning the cursor on each item.

CLICKING
You can select an item by positioning the rectangular pointer or the tip of the arrow over the item and quickly pressing and releasing the left-hand mouse button. This action is known as clicking.

1 Click on the *Directory Tree* title bar. The title bar becomes selected (highlighted) to show that the area is active.

```
          Directory Tree
→[-] C:\
    ├─[ ] DOS
    ├─[ ] HOBBIES
    ├─[ ] OLD_DOS.1
    ├─[+] WINDOWS
    └─[+] WINWORD
```

2 Now select the CONFIG.SYS file in the file list area. You will see both the title bar of this area and the filename become highlighted. Meanwhile, the *Directory Tree* title bar is deselected.

DRAGGING
To drag, you press the left-hand mouse button and hold it down while moving the mouse. You can use either a dragging action or a clicking action to select commands from the drop-down menus. Dragging is also used for actions like moving files from one directory to another.

1 Move your pointer over the menu name *File* in the menu bar. Press down the left-hand mouse button and a drop-down menu will appear. Keep holding down the mouse button.

2 Move your mouse down the mouse pad and you will see the pointer scroll down the menu, high-lighting each item as it goes. Without letting go of the mouse button, scroll back up until the pointer is in the MS-DOS Shell title bar. Then release the button.

I Have a Mouse But I Don't Have a Pointer!
If you can't see a mouse cursor on your screen, you need to run the special program that is supplied with your mouse. If it's installed properly, you only need to type in the command MOUSE at the command prompt before you run the MS-DOS Shell. See page 112 in the Reference Section for more information.

Can I Get Around Without a Mouse?
If you don't have a mouse, you can use certain keys to move around the window. The Tab key will move the highlight to different areas; the direction keys move the highlight within these areas. The Enter key carries out commands once they are highlighted.

93

Choosing a Menu Command

Commands in the Shell are contained in drop-down menus hidden under the menu names in the menu bar. Clicking on a menu name reveals a drop-down menu. If you are using the keyboard, press Alt once; the *File* menu name will be highlighted. Use the Right direction key to highlight each menu name in turn. Once a menu name is highlighted, press Enter to display the drop-down menu. You can press the Esc key to close the menu again.

Want Help?
If you need assistance while in the Shell, try using the *Help* menu. For example, the *Keyboard* command in the *Help* menu explains how to use the keyboard to get around the Shell. Many of the dialog boxes that appear when you select commands also have a *Help* option that you can access. In addition, you can always press F1 for context-sensitive help.

TWO VIEWS
The Shell uses either text or graphics to show the directories and files stored on your disks. The first time you run the MS-DOS Shell, the display appears in text mode. Let's change the display to the graphics mode.

Changing Your Display

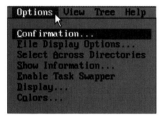

1 Click on the menu name *Options,* and a menu drops down. The first command in this menu, *Confirmation*, will be highlighted.

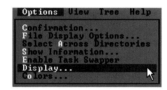

2 Move the mouse pointer to the *Display* command and click the mouse button. If you are using the keyboard, use the Down direction key to highlight the *Display* command, and then press Enter.

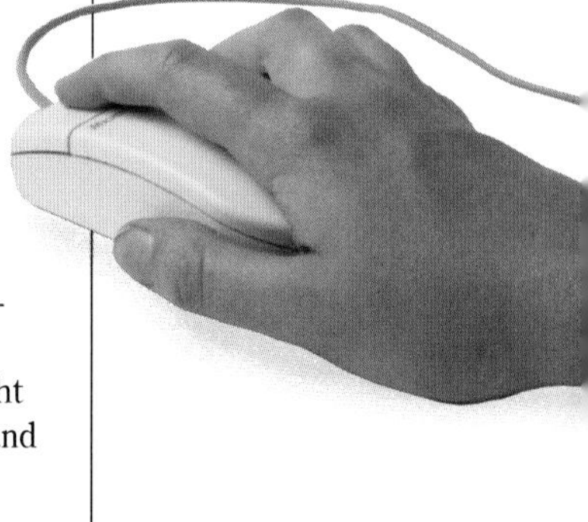

3 A dialog box listing all the available display modes appears. If you have a mouse, click on the down scroll arrow at the right side of the box until the *Graphics 30 lines Medium Resolution 1* line is shown. Select the line by clicking on it. If you don't have a mouse, use the Down direction key to move to the line.

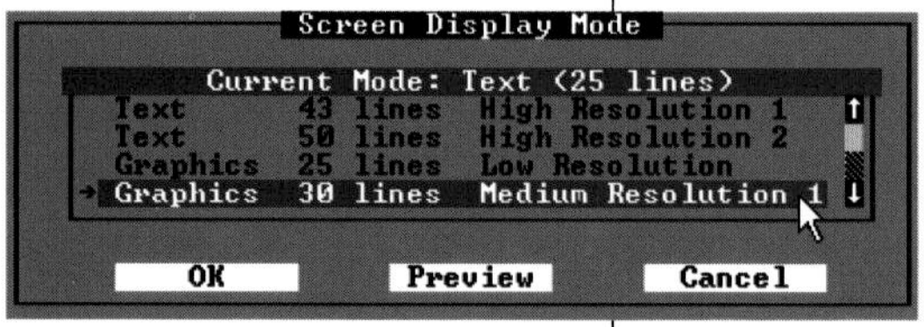

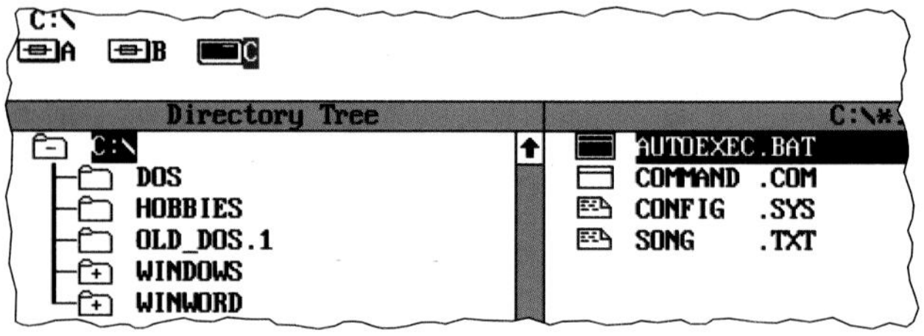

4 Press Enter. Your screen will briefly go blank and then reappear in graphics mode, as shown at left.

The Directory Tree

The *Directory Tree* area on the left-hand side of the screen shows how all the directories on a disk are organized. Each directory is represented by a little picture of a folder. The root directory is shown at the top, with the subdirectories of the root directory branching off from a vertical line below it.

PLUS AND MINUS

Directories containing subdirectories have a plus sign in the center of the folder. With your mouse or keyboard, select a directory that contains a plus sign, and then click on the plus sign with the mouse, or press the Plus key on your keyboard. The directory tree display will change to show the subdirectories stored within that parent directory. At the same time, a minus sign will appear in the center of the parent directory's folder. Press the Minus key, or click again with the mouse pointer on the minus sign, and the subdirectories will disappear back into their parent.

Sometimes a subdirectory itself will have a plus sign on its folder, indicating that it contains its own subdirectories. You can display the whole directory tree structure under one parent directory by selecting the parent directory with mouse or keyboard and then pressing the Asterisk key.

A Parent Directory
The plus sign in the center of the WINDOWS directory folder icon shows that it contains subdirectories.

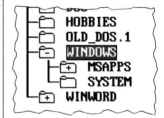

Subdirectories
Clicking on the plus sign with the mouse will show the subdirectories stored in the WINDOWS directory.

Hot Keys
When you press the Alt key, you will see that the first letter of each of the menu names is underlined. These are the menu names' "hot keys." Pressing the Alt key and a hot key together will give you fast access to the drop-down menu beneath a menu name.

File Icons
Here, the different icons in the file list area on the right-hand side of the screen represent the different types of files present in the DOS directory.

SELECTING FILES

Activate the file list area by pressing the Tab key until the file list area title bar is highlighted or by moving the mouse into the area and clicking the left-hand button once. The files now listed in the file area are those stored in the directory that's highlighted in the *Directory Tree* area of the screen. Displaying files in this way is the same as using the MS-DOS command CD and then typing DIR at the command prompt, except that it's much easier and more visual.

The different types of files are represented by different pictures. A program file (one with an EXE, COM, or BAT extension) is shown as a rectangle with a line near the top. All other files are represented by a picture, or icon, that looks like a piece of paper with the corner turned over.

One Click Is Enough!
When selecting a menu, command, or the name of a file, make sure you click only once on the mouse button. Double-clicking is a convention used to initiate some actions, so if you click twice by mistake, you might find the MS-DOS Shell reacting in a way you didn't intend. You'll learn more about double-clicking on page 97.

Copying Files

Now that you know how to select a file in a particular
directory using your mouse, let's copy a file from one
directory into another. You should have a file called
README.TXT in your DOS directory. You are going
to copy this file into your root directory using
either your mouse or your keyboard.

How to Copy Files Using a Mouse

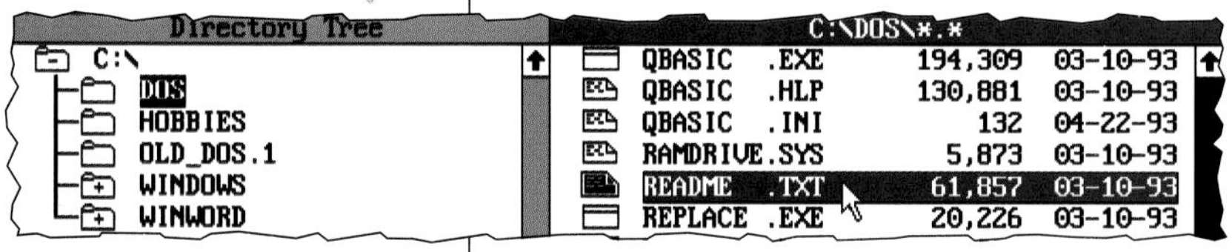

1 In the *Directory Tree* area, select the
DOS directory. Then activate the file list
area and scroll down the list of files until the
README.TXT file appears. Select this file
and keep holding down the mouse button.
Now hold down the Ctrl key.

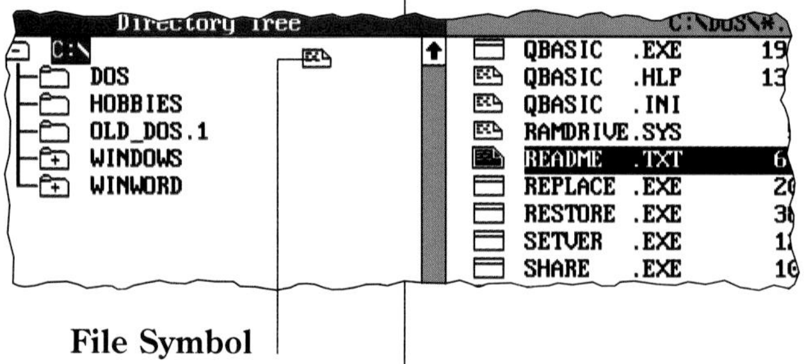

2 With the Ctrl key and the left
mouse button both held down,
drag the pointer into the *Directory
Tree* area. The pointer will change
into a file symbol. Move it to the C:\
at the top of the directory tree; the
C:\ will become highlighted.

File Symbol

3 Let go of the mouse button and the Ctrl key.
A window will appear asking
if you are sure you want to
copy the file. Answer yes by
clicking on the *Yes* button.

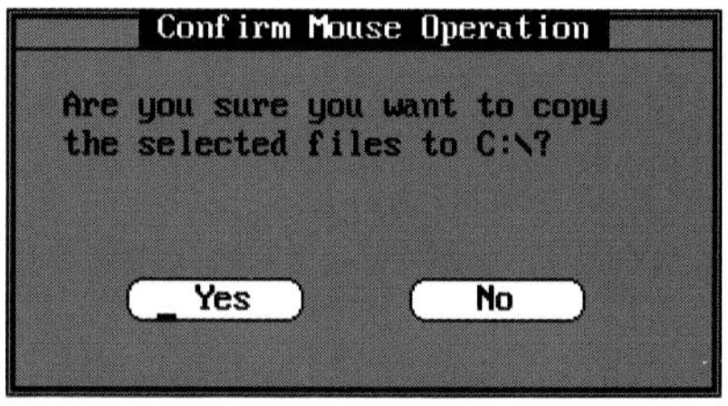

Confirm Mouse Operation

Are you sure you want to copy
the selected files to C:\?

[Yes]   [No]

How to Copy Files Using the Keyboard

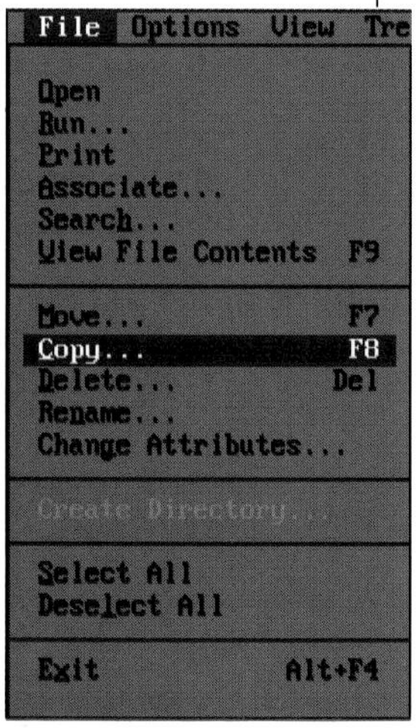

1 Press the Tab key until
the *Directory Tree* area is
active, then press the Down
direction key to highlight
the DOS directory. Press
the Tab key until the file list
area is active, and then use
the Down direction key to
highlight the README.TXT
file. Now press Alt-F to display the *File* menu. Use the
Down direction key to
choose the *Copy* command,
and then press Enter.

2 The *Copy File* dialog box appears, displaying in
the *From* text box the name of the file you are
copying. The *To* text box shows the highlighted
pathname of the file. In the *To* text box, type the
name of the directory into which you want to move
the file — C:\, as shown below. Now press Enter.

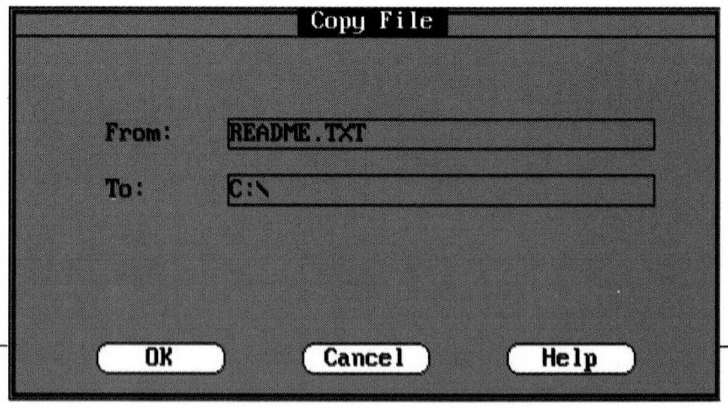

Copy File

From: README.TXT

To: C:\

[OK]   [Cancel]   [Help]

File   Options   View   Tre

Open
Run...
Print
Associate...
Search...
View File Contents   F9

Move...   F7
Copy...   F8
Delete...   Del
Rename...
Change Attributes...

Create Directory...

Select All
Deselect All

Exit   Alt+F4

Running Programs

You can run programs from the Shell without going back to the command prompt. Let's run the Editor, a program that you used in Chapter 4 (see page 68) to create a file. To run the Editor using a mouse, you need to learn a new skill — double-clicking. A double-click consists of two clicks in rapid succession on the left-hand button. The first few times you try this, you might not click fast enough. Your software expects the two clicks to follow each other closely; if you take too long, it will treat your attempts as two single clicks.

How to Run the Editor Program

1 Select the DOS directory in the *Directory Tree* area, then scroll down the list in the file area until you reach the EDIT.COM file. Move the pointer over this file entry and double-click; alternatively, use the keyboard to select EDIT.COM, and then press Enter.

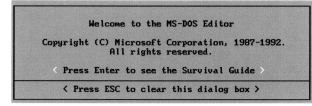

```
Welcome to the MS-DOS Editor

Copyright (C) Microsoft Corporation, 1987-1992.
           All rights reserved.

    < Press Enter to see the Survival Guide >

    < Press ESC to clear this dialog box >
```

2 The Editor program will run. Press Esc to clear the screen. Exit the Editor as described on page 69, step 5.

You will also see the Editor program listed in the program list area at the bottom of the screen. You can launch it from there by double-clicking on its name, then pressing Enter when the *File to Edit* box appears.

Viewing Other Disks

You can use the MS-DOS Shell to view and manipulate directories and files stored on other disks. To see the contents of a floppy disk, insert it into the correct disk drive, then select the floppy disk drive letter in the top section of the screen. The file and directory display will show the contents of the floppy disk drive. Select the disk drive letter C to get back to the hard drive.

To Exit the MS-DOS Shell

To leave the MS-DOS Shell and return to the standard command prompt, drop down the File *menu and then choose the last option,* Exit.

How Do I Move Files?

If you have a mouse, you can also use the dragging action to move files. The steps are the same as those used to copy a file except that you don't press the Ctrl key. To move files by using the keyboard, choose *Move* from the *File* menu.

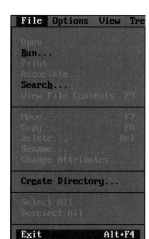

Multiple Moves
You can select several files in the file list area at once by holding down the Ctrl key and clicking with the mouse on each filename in turn to highlight them. You can then move or copy all the files in unison.

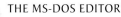

The MS-DOS Editor

Y OU WORKED WITH THE MS-DOS Editor in Chapter 4 when you
used it to create and save the file RHYME.TXT. You can also use
the MS-DOS Editor to modify files. It lets you move selected text
from one location to another or delete whole paragraphs. Before using
the Editor, first let's open a text file. Open README.TXT, which you
copied to your root directory using the MS-DOS Shell.

Opening a File in the Editor

Type EDIT \README.TXT at the command prompt;
make sure that you type the full pathname of the file
you want to edit. Press Enter and the Editor window
will appear on your screen with the top portion of the
README.TXT file displayed.

It's best to imagine the MS-DOS Editor as a viewer
over a document that you can see only one section at a
time. This document can be up to 255 characters wide
and as long as you want, but the workspace you see on
your screen — the Editor window — is limited to 78
characters in width and 21 rows in height.

Scroll Bar
*Clicking on a scroll
bar will scroll the text
one screenful at a time.*

Keyboard Moves
The direction keys
move your insertion
point up, down, left,
or right; the Home
and End keys move
it to the beginning or
end of a line; the
PgUp and PgDn keys
move the text one
screenful at a time.

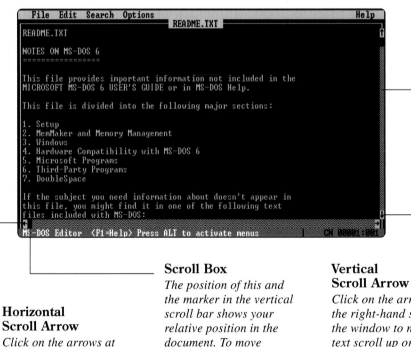

Scroll Box
*The position of this and
the marker in the vertical
scroll bar shows your
relative position in the
document. To move
quickly around the text,
drag the scroll box along
the scroll bar to the part
of the file you want to see.*

**Vertical
Scroll Arrow**
*Click on the arrows at
the right-hand side of
the window to make the
text scroll up or down
one line at a time.*

**Horizontal
Scroll Arrow**
*Click on the arrows at
the bottom of the window
to scroll your text to the
right or left one charac-
ter width at a time.*

Messed up a File?
If you make a mess of
your editing, choose the
Exit command from the
File menu. Before
closing your file, MS-
DOS will ask you if you
want to save the loaded
file; choose the *No*
option to ignore any
changes you have made
since the last time you
saved the file.

Editing Techniques

You can highlight, or select, words or blocks of text by placing the insertion point at the beginning of the first word, holding down the mouse button, and moving the pointer to the end of the word or block of text. You can delete a whole section of text if you highlight it and then press the Delete key.

Highlighting also lets you move sections of text. In the README.TXT file, let's move the fourth word — "important" — in the first sentence so that it becomes the second word in the sentence.

Cut and Paste

1 Highlight the word "important" with your mouse (include the space before "important" as well). If you do not have a mouse, you can highlight text by holding down the Shift key and pressing a direction key.

2 Choose the *Cut* command from the *Edit* menu.

3 The highlighted word disappears but is saved in a special area of memory called the Clipboard.

4 Use your mouse or the Left direction key to move the insertion point to the place you want the word to appear — just after the word "This" in the first line — and then choose the *Paste* command from the *Edit* menu. The word "important" will reappear at the insertion point.

The Search Menu

The *Find* command in the *Search* menu opens a dialog box that lets you search text for a specific word or a string of text. You type the word or text into the *Find What* box. If you want the Editor to match the capitalization style of your word when it does a search, check the *Match Upper/Lowercase* box by clicking on it with your mouse or by pressing Tab and then the Spacebar. If you don't want to identify words that might be contained within larger words, check the *Whole Word* box. Click *OK* to close the dialog box, and the first occurrence of the word will be highlighted.

The *Change* command in the *Search* menu opens a dialog box that lets you replace one text string with another. Type the text string you want to change in the *Find What* text box, then move to the *Change To* text box and type the replacement word. To replace all matching words with the new word, click on the *Change All* button or use Tab to move to this button and press Enter.

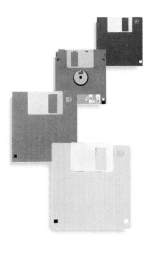

Backup and Restore

ACKUPS ARE COPIES of your files that are kept on separate storage media, such as floppy disks or backup tape. Backing up your files and directories protects against both human error and loss of data if your machine breaks down. Data can be lost through hard disk failure and the accidental deletion of a file, but if you make regular backups you can quickly and easily restore the files using the MS-DOS program Microsoft Backup.

Floppy disks are the most common medium for backing up files. If you have large amounts of data to back up you will need a large stack of floppy disks, for example, at least seven high-capacity 3½-inch disks if you want to back up 10MB of data. A tape back-up unit or a removable hard disk are much quicker and more convenient backup devices, but tape backup is not supported by MS-DOS Backup and this method also requires the use of special programs.

**Removable
Hard Disk Drive**

Alert Box

The Alert *box asks you to configure the Backup utility for your PC.*

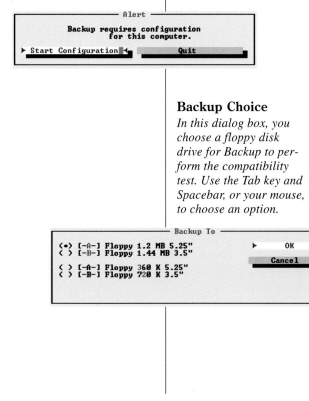

Backup Choice

In this dialog box, you choose a floppy disk drive for Backup to perform the compatibility test. Use the Tab key and Spacebar, or your mouse, to choose an option.

Setting Up Backup

The first time you type MSBACKUP at the command prompt, an *Alert* box will appear on your screen telling you to configure the Backup program for your PC. Make sure you have two blank floppy disks on hand, and then press Enter to start the configuration. A window titled *Video and Mouse Configuration* appears. Press Enter to tell your PC that the setup is correct. The *Floppy Drive Change Line Test* screen will then appear. Press Enter to start the test. When the *Backup Devices* window appears, press Enter again and you will see your PC performing a series of tests.

When the *Floppy Disk Compatibility Test* screen appears, press Enter. A series of windows will flash on your screen. When the *Alert* box tells you that your PC will pause to let you select a floppy drive, press Enter. A *Backup To* dialog box appears next, with drive A selected; click on *OK*, or choose the drive you will use and press Enter. You'll be asked to insert the first blank floppy disk into your chosen drive. Do so and continue the test by pressing Enter. Later, you will be asked for the second disk. When the program has saved data to the floppy disks, you'll see a *Backup Complete* window. Press Enter and you'll be asked to insert the first disk again. Backup runs a comparison test to check that the backup has been successful; if it was not, contact an expert.

CONFIGURING YOUR DRIVES

After completing the compatibility test, you still need to configure the drives you will be using before performing your first backup. Follow steps 1 and 2 below if you are not already at the *Configure* screen.

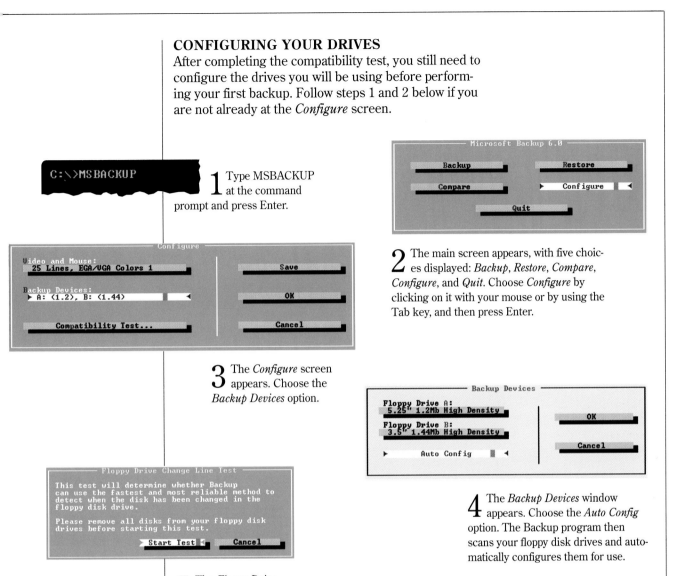

1 Type MSBACKUP at the command prompt and press Enter.

2 The main screen appears, with five choices displayed: *Backup, Restore, Compare, Configure,* and *Quit.* Choose *Configure* by clicking on it with your mouse or by using the Tab key, and then press Enter.

3 The *Configure* screen appears. Choose the *Backup Devices* option.

4 The *Backup Devices* window appears. Choose the *Auto Config* option. The Backup program then scans your floppy disk drives and automatically configures them for use.

5 The *Floppy Drive Change Line Test* screen appears and tells you to remove any floppy disks from the disk drives. Check that your floppy drives are empty, and then press Enter to start the test.

Once the test is complete, choose *OK* in the *Backup Devices* box. You will be returned to the *Configure* screen; choose the *Save* option so that your PC will use your chosen configuration every time you do a backup.

Three Paths to Protection

There are three types of backup: A full backup copies all the files you select; an incremental backup backs up new files or files whose contents have changed since the previous full or incremental backup; a differential backup backs up all files that have changed since your last full backup. A differential backup can be used to replace a series of incremental backups or to update files from the previous differential backup.

How Often Should I Back Up?
A backup cycle begins with a comprehensive backup. You should do one full backup every week or so if you use your PC heavily and supplement this with incremental or differential backups as often as you make changes to files.

How to Back Up a Directory

Now that you have set up your Microsoft Backup program, you can use it to make regular backups of your important files. Before you do so, make sure you have a supply of blank floppy disks ready. You don't have to format the floppy disks because the backup program will do that automatically.

During the course of this book, you've created, copied to, and deleted files from a directory called HOBBIES, and this directory still contains some files. Let's back up the contents of the HOBBIES directory onto a floppy disk.

Backing Up a Directory onto a Floppy Disk

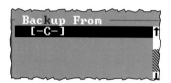

1 Start the Backup program by typing MSBACKUP at the command prompt. Choose the *Backup* option, and the *Backup* window will appear. On the left is the *Backup From* box, which lists the hard disks on your system, in this example drive C. Click on the drive C option, or press the Tab key, and it will become highlighted.

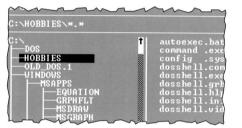

2 Press Enter. The Backup program spends a few seconds looking at all the files stored on your hard disk, then displays a *Select Backup Files* window with a directory tree on the left and a file list on the right. Use the Down direction key to move the highlight bar to the HOBBIES directory; keep scrolling down if you can't see it listed.

3 With the HOBBIES directory highlighted, press the Spacebar. This tells the program to select this directory to back up; all the files in the HOBBIES directory (listed on the right) will now be checked. Press Enter, and you will be returned to the main *Backup* window.

4 Insert a floppy disk into drive A and choose *Start Backup* with your mouse or by using the Tab key and pressing Enter. An *Alert* dialog box will appear asking you to insert the first blank floppy disk. Because you have already done this, press Enter. A window will then inform you of the backup progress.

```
┌──────── Backup Complete ────────┐
│                                  │
│  Selected   files:         9     │
│  Backed up files:          9     │
│  Skipped:                  0     │
│                                  │
│  Disks:                    1     │
│  Bytes:              157,716     │
│                                  │
│  Total Time:            0:26     │
│  Your Time:             0:17     │
│  Backup Time:           0:09     │
│                                  │
│  KBytes Per Min:       1,046     │
│  Compression:            1.9     │
│                                  │
│        ►    OK    ◄               │
└──────────────────────────────────┘
```

5 When the backup is finished, a *Backup Complete* window will appear; press Enter, and Backup will display its main program window.

How to Restore a File

If you delete a file by mistake and can't retrieve it with the UNDELETE command, you'll need to recover the backup copy from the floppy disks to restore the file to your hard disk. You can locate the file with the aid of the backup catalog — a special file that is created each time you do a backup.

Let's deliberately delete a file. You've just backed up your HOBBIES directory, so choose a file from there. Quit the Backup program to return to the command prompt, then type DEL\HOBBIES\CONFIG.SYS and press Enter to delete the CONFIG.SYS file in your HOBBIES directory (the original of this file is in the root directory). Now type MSBACKUP and press Enter. In the *Backup* program window, choose *Restore* and the *Restore* window will appear.

How Many Disks do I Need?
If you're not sure how many floppy disks you'll need for a backup, after you choose *Start Backup* (step 4 on page 102) look in the bottom right-hand corner of your screen, at the *Backup Set Information* section. You'll see an estimate of the number of disks you'll need.

Restoring a File

1 The *Backup Set Catalog* option in the *Restore* window contains the filename of the last catalog name recorded on your hard disk. Your CONFIG.SYS file will be in this catalog. Put the floppy disk containing your backup into the disk drive.

2 Choose *Select Files* and press Enter to display the *Select Restore Files* window. Scroll through the directory names on the left of the screen until the highlight bar reaches the HOBBIES directory. Then press the Tab key to move into the list of files on the right. Use the Down direction key to highlight the CONFIG.SYS file, and then press the Spacebar; a check mark will appear next to the CONFIG.SYS file. Press Enter, and you will be returned to the *Restore* window.

```
:\HOBBIES\*.*
:\                              autoexec.bat
├─DOS                           command .exe
│  └─AUTOEXEC                 √ config   .sys
→HOBBIES              ◄         dosshell.com
├─OLD_DOS.1                     dosshell.exe
├─WINDOWS                       dosshell.grb
│  ├─MSAPPS                     dosshell.hlp
│  │  ├─EQUATION                dosshell.ini
│  │  ├─GRPHFLT                 dosshell.vid
│  │  ├─MSDRAW
```

3 The *Select Files* box now has *1 file selected for restore* next to it. Use the Tab key to choose the *Start Restore* button and press Enter.

4 The window will change to give you information on the restoration, and an *Alert* box will ask you to insert the disk with your backup files into drive A. You have already done this, so just press Enter.

```
                    ─ Alert ─
Insert diskette # 1 of backup set CC30426A.FUL
               into drive A.

    ►   Continue  ◄       Cancel Restore
```

When the *Restore Complete* box appears, press Enter to return to the main *Backup* window. Choose *Quit* to return to the command prompt, and then type the command DIR\HOBBIES to check that the file CONFIG.SYS is back in your HOBBIES directory.

DoubleSpace

T HE AMOUNT OF DATA that can be stored on a floppy disk or hard disk is determined by the disk's capacity. If your PC is equipped with a 40MB hard disk, it can normally store 40 million bytes (one byte is equal to one character of text). That might sound like a lot, but it can be used up very quickly by modern computer programs. MS-DOS 6 includes a program called DoubleSpace that will double the storage capacity of your hard disk or a floppy disk by compressing the data stored on it.

Normally when you save a file, it is saved straight to disk. Once you set up DoubleSpace, when you save a file it will be compressed as it is being saved. When you next read the file from your hard disk, Double-Space will automatically decompress the file as you read it. It does this invisibly — you'll never know it's there — so you can continue working as normal.

Always Back Up First
Before setting up DoubleSpace, back up all the important files on your disk. Double-Space saves files in a special format, so you may want a backup copy of your files without the Double-Space compression.

Setting Up DoubleSpace

Before setting up DoubleSpace, make a backup of your important files. (See "Backup and Restore" on pages 100 to 103.) To set up DoubleSpace you must be at the command prompt, so ensure that you have left the MS-DOS Shell program or any other program, such as Windows.

1 Type DBLSPACE at the command prompt and press Enter. Press Enter again at the *Welcome* screen.

```
Welcome to DoubleSpace Setup
```

2 The next screen asks you to make a choice between the *Express Setup* or *Custom Setup* option. Express Setup installs and configures Doublespace for you. Custom Setup lets you modify how DoubleSpace works. Choose the *Express Setup* option by pressing Enter.

```
Express Setup (recommended)
Custom Setup
```

```
DoubleSpace is ready to compress drive C. This will take 42
minutes.
```

3 A screen appears that de- scribes the setup process and lists an estimated time of duration and a warning that your PC will restart during the process. A message tells you to press C if you want to com- press the current drive — in this case, drive C. Press C and the setup program will run.

During the disk compression process, the *Microsoft DoubleSpace Setup* screen will inform you of how the compression is progressing. Once your existing files have been compressed, your PC will be reset and you'll be back at the command prompt — with a hard disk that offers twice as much free disk space as it did be- fore you set up DoubleSpace.

DoubleSpace Already Set Up?
If you don't see the setup options when you run DBLSPACE but instead see the graphical DoubleSpace screen, DoubleSpace is already set up on your system and you won't need to follow steps 1 to 3.

Floppy Disk Compression

You can also use DoubleSpace to compress your floppy disks. They must be formatted and have a minimum of 650KB free space for the DoubleSpace program to work. If you transfer data from one PC to another with a compressed floppy disk, both machines must have DoubleSpace set up.

To compress a floppy disk, put the disk in the correct drive of a PC that has already had DoubleSpace set up. Type DBLSPACE at the command prompt. Press Enter to get to the DoubleSpace screen.

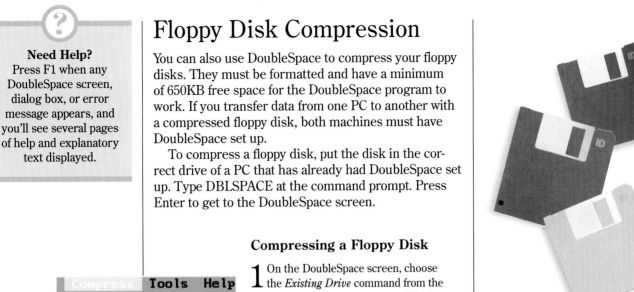

Need Help?
Press F1 when any DoubleSpace screen, dialog box, or error message appears, and you'll see several pages of help and explanatory text displayed.

Compressing a Floppy Disk

1 On the DoubleSpace screen, choose the *Existing Drive* command from the *Compress* menu. After a pause, while the program scans your PC to see what drives are available, a list of the drives that can be used to compress floppy disks appears.

```
Compress   Tools   Help

Existing Drive...
Create New Drive...
```

2 Select the drive your floppy disk is in, and then press Enter. The program will tell you which disk it is about to compress. Check that you have chosen the correct drive, and then press C to continue.

Drive	Current Free Space	Projected Free Space
A	1.3 MB	2.6 MB

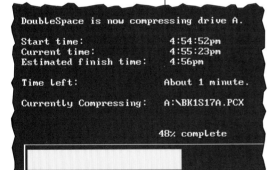

```
DoubleSpace is now compressing drive A.

Start time:             4:54:52pm
Current time:           4:55:23pm
Estimated finish time:  4:56pm

Time left:              About 1 minute.

Currently Compressing:  A:\BK1S17A.PCX

                        48% complete
```

3 The screen will change to show information about the progress of the compression; when it is finished, you will be back at the main DoubleSpace screen, from where you can exit the program.

USING A COMPRESSED FLOPPY DISK

Before using a compressed floppy disk you have to inform MS-DOS that the floppy disk is compressed. To do this, simply insert the disk in drive A or B, type DBLSPACE /MOUNT A: (or MOUNT B:), and press Enter. You can then use the disk as normal.

How Much Free Disk Space is Left?
When you use the DIR command in the root directory, the very last line of the display will show you how much free disk space you have left on your disk. Try doing this before and after using DoubleSpace and you will see how much more space you have on your disk after the compression has been performed.

Anti-Virus Utility

I N ALMOST THE SAME WAY that biological viruses affect humans, computer *viruses* can infect your personal computer. Viruses are tiny programs that can copy themselves onto floppy or hard disks, spreading from machine to machine. Fortunately, most PC viruses won't do anything worse than cause your computer to beep or display a message; however, some can wreck files or corrupt data.

Avoiding Trouble

You should play it safe by buying and using only software that is shrink-wrapped, which shows that it hasn't been used elsewhere. Other software that is supplied by user groups or warehouses is usually checked for viruses before being passed on, so these might be reasonable sources as well. Be most wary of illegally copied programs because they are a common means of spreading viruses.

Computer Checkup

MS-DOS 6 includes a special program that scans your hard disk or floppy disk to examine whether any virus program has invaded. If a problem is found, the virus is automatically removed. Follow a positive computer health routine by scanning your machine regularly to check that the disks and files are kept clean.

SCANNING YOUR HARD DISK
Follow the steps on the next page to keep your hard disk or floppy disks in robust health. It may seem like a nuisance, but you will find that putting in a little regular effort goes a long way toward keeping your computer in peak form. As with your own body, preventative care is worth the trouble.

If any viruses are detected by the Anti-Virus program, the infected file is cleared and the scan continues to the next file. Once the disk has been fully scanned, a window entitled *Viruses Detected and Cleaned* is displayed summarizing all the information. If you need help while using the Anti-Virus utility, press F1; you can also press F9 to obtain a list of the viruses the program will detect.

Continuous Protection
You can monitor virus activity by enabling another small program called VSAFE. To do so, type in VSAFE after the command prompt and press Enter. VSAFE will then monitor your computer continuously for virus activity.

Use Windows?
If you use Microsoft Windows, you can run a Windows version of the Anti-Virus program. To start the program, double-click on the *Microsoft Tools* group icon, then on the *Anti-Virus* icon in *Program Manager*.

`C:\>MSAV`

1 Type MSAV (which stands for Microsoft Anti-Virus) at the command prompt, and then press Enter.

2 The *Main Menu* window is displayed with five main options on the left-hand side of the screen. Click on *Detect & Clean* with the mouse. Alternatively, use the Down direction key to move to the *Detect & Clean* option and press Enter.

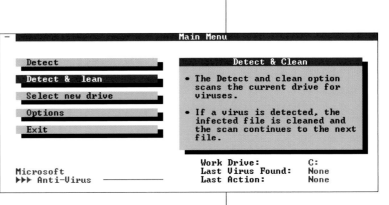

```
 -                          Main Menu

    Detect
    Detect &  lean                          Detect & Clean
    Select new drive              • The Detect and clean option
    Options                         scans the current drive for
    Exit                            viruses.
                                  • If a virus is detected, the
                                    infected file is cleaned and
                                    the scan continues to the next
                                    file.

 Microsoft                        Work Drive:          C:
 ▶▶▶ Anti-Virus                   Last Virus Found:    None
                                  Last Action:         None
```

3 While the disk is being checked for any virus infections, you can watch the percentage bars fill as the scan is made. Because the program looks at every file stored on the disk, this examination could take 5 to 10 minutes.

```
           Detect & Clean

 0%                        100%
           27%
 Directories to scan:        13

 0%                        100%
           99%
 Files in current dir:        1
```

SCANNING YOUR FLOPPY DISK

If you want to scan a floppy disk to check that it is not carrying any viruses, you can use the MSAV program to do so.

1 Type MSAV to start the Anti-Virus program. In the *Main Menu* window, use the direction keys to move to the *Select new drive* option. Press Enter.

```
 -                          Main Menu

    Detect
    Detect & Clean                       Select new drive
    elect new drive               • This option displays the drive
    Options                         line so you can select a
    Exit                            different drive to scan and/or
                                    clean.


 Microsoft                        Work Drive:          C:
 ▶▶▶ Anti-Virus                   Last Virus Found:    None
                                  Last Action:         None
```

2 The top left-hand corner of the screen will show the drive letters. On most PCs there will be only three options, the hard drive C and two floppy drives. Use the direction keys to pick the drive you want to scan, and then press Enter — or you can click on the disk drive with your mouse pointer.

3 Use your direction keys or mouse to choose *Detect & Clean*. MS-DOS will now scan the floppy disk as it did the hard disk.

Defragmentation

A S YOU SAVE NEW FILES on your hard disk, the disk will gradually fill up. When you delete a file, MS-DOS doesn't reorganize the disk; instead, a gap is created, and MS-DOS will fill this with the next file you save. If the new file is too big for the gap, MS-DOS will store as much as possible in the gap and store the rest in the next convenient area of the hard disk.

After a few months of normal use, your hard disk is likely to be full of fragmented files spread out like a mosaic in different areas. This scattering of data will slow down both MS-DOS and any other programs you use. Instead of being able to retrieve a single file, MS-DOS will have to carefully pick out parts of the file from a variety of locations.

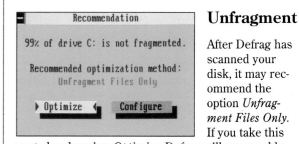

Creating Order
The jumbled mosaic of colors suggests the way files become fragmented on your disk. The neater pattern of colors shows how Defrag condenses the files into better order.

Organizing Your Hard Disk

To produce a neatly organized hard disk in which all the files are stored optimally, you can use an MS-DOS defragmentation utility called Defrag. This program is stored as a file called DEFRAG.EXE in the DOS directory of your hard disk.

If you want to speed up access to your hard disk, it is a good idea to try running the Defrag program every couple of months. This will result in a hard disk that stores files in an orderly fashion. Before you run Defrag, make a backup copy of your important data (see "Backup and Restore" on pages 100 to 103).

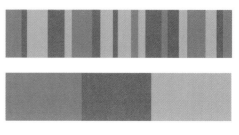

Unfragment

After Defrag has scanned your disk, it may recommend the option *Unfragment Files Only*. If you take this route by choosing *Optimize*, Defrag will reassemble the parts of each fragmented file but will not fill all gaps. Alternatively, press F1 to learn how to perform a full optimization. For more information, type HELP DEFRAG at the command prompt.

Steps to Defragment Your Hard Disk

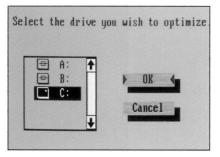

1 Type DEFRAG at the command prompt and press Enter.

2 The main screen appears and asks you to choose which disk you want to optimize. Choose your hard disk, drive C. Press Enter, or click on *OK* with your mouse.

3 The Defrag program scans the disk drive, then recommends an option for defragmenting the disk — either *Full Optimization* or *Unfragment Files Only*. Click on *Optimize* or press Enter to choose the recommended option.

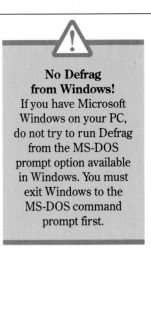

No Defrag from Windows!
If you have Microsoft Windows on your PC, do not try to run Defrag from the MS-DOS prompt option available in Windows. You must exit Windows to the MS-DOS command prompt first.

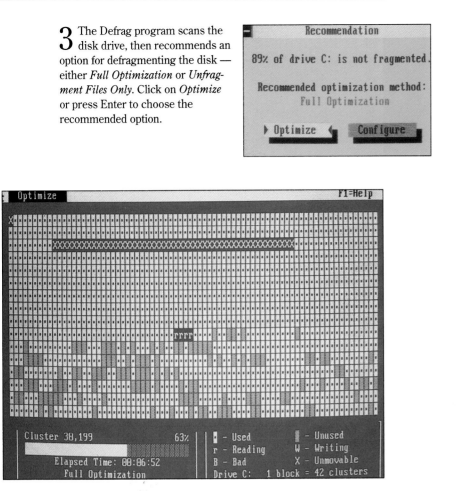

4 Defrag now starts to reorganize the disk drive. This process may take from a few seconds to half an hour or more. A graphical display shows how the defragmentation is progressing.

5 When the mosaic of different elements on your screen has been reorganized, the screen message *Finished condensing* appears. Press Enter.

How Does It Work?
Defragmentation works by reading one file at a time. Parts of the file are retrieved from scattered locations and then saved again in one chunk.

6 The message shown at right then appears. If you do not want to defragment another disk, choose *Exit DEFRAG*.

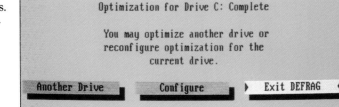

Undelete

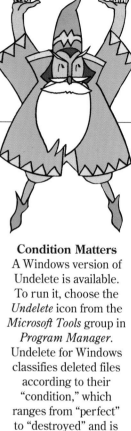

ACCIDENTS HAPPEN, but fortunately MS-DOS 6 has a remedy for one kind: the Undelete program recovers deleted material that you want back. There are three levels of overall undelete protection available, and the level you choose may well determine how successful you will be in regaining data. The standard level, which was explained on page 73, is available automatically when you switch on your machine. The other levels are activated by using the UNDELETE command and adding a switch.

Three Levels of Cover

The three levels of protection offered by MS-DOS 6 are Delete Sentry, Delete Tracker, and standard.

▧ Delete Sentry offers the highest level of protection and needs a small amount of disk space and memory — about 13.5KB. When you delete a file, MS-DOS moves the file to a hidden SENTRY directory. If you then use the UNDELETE command, MS-DOS will move the file back to its original place. The SENTRY directory is limited to only 7 percent of your hard disk space; if your deletions exceed this, MS-DOS will eliminate the oldest files to make space for more recent file deletions.

▧ Delete Tracker offers a lower level of protection than Delete Sentry. It requires the same amount of memory as Sentry but less disk space. A hidden file, PCTRACKER.DEL, records the full name and location of each deleted file. You can recover a deleted file totally using the UNDELETE command provided no other file has been placed over the same location. If MS-DOS has placed another file over the same location you might still be able to partially recover the file.

▧ The standard level of protection is the lowest and does not require any memory or disk space. You can recover a deleted file using the UNDELETE command if no other file has been placed over the same location. If another file has been placed over this location, you may be unable to recover any part of the deleted file.

Choosing Delete Sentry or Delete Tracker

```
C:\>UNDELETE /s
```

1 To activate the Delete Sentry level of protection, simply type in UNDELETE /s at the command prompt and press Enter.

```
C:\>UNDELETE /tc
```

2 To activate Delete Tracker, add the /t switch and the drive you want to protect after the command. For example, to use Delete Tracker on drive C, type UNDELETE /tc and press Enter.

Condition Matters
A Windows version of Undelete is available. To run it, choose the *Undelete* icon from the *Microsoft Tools* group in *Program Manager*. Undelete for Windows classifies deleted files according to their "condition," which ranges from "perfect" to "destroyed" and is a rating of their likelihood of being successfully recovered.

How Does Undelete Work?
When you delete a file, it isn't erased immediately from your hard disk. The file is simply "lined up" for deletion once space is needed for another file being created or expanded.

Reference Section

*This section provides additional information
to help you get the most out of your PC. It includes
a guide to installing MS-DOS, a listing of commands
and error messages, and a description of different types
of software. The description of MS-DOS and memory and
the explanation of batch files offer information for
improving your PC's performance and making
it easier to use. At the back of the Reference
Section you'll find a useful glossary of
technical terms and an index.*

INSTALLING MS-DOS 6 • SOFTWARE GUIDE
MS-DOS AND MEMORY • BATCH FILES
WHAT IS A NETWORK? • MS-DOS COMMANDS
ERROR MESSAGES • MY PC DOESN'T WORK
GLOSSARY • INDEX

Installing MS-DOS 6

THERE ARE TWO WAYS to install MS-DOS 6: by upgrading to the new version or by performing a complete installation. Most users will upgrade from an earlier version of MS-DOS; this method is explained below. If you have just bought a new PC and MS-DOS has not been installed on the hard disk, skip the first section of this page and follow the instructions on the right.

Upgrading from an Earlier Version of MS-DOS

Before upgrading, make a complete backup of all your important files and programs. For the upgrade, you'll need two blank floppy disks that fit into drive A and the MS-DOS 6 installation disks. MS-DOS uses the blank disks as uninstall disks to keep a record of the files on your hard disk; if something goes wrong, they can be used to recover any lost files. Turn on your PC and begin the upgrade.

How to Upgrade to MS-DOS 6

1 Insert the Setup Disk 1 into drive A or B and then type A:SETUP or B:SETUP at the command prompt. Press Enter.

2 The Setup program will run. MS-DOS will display instructions on the screen to guide you through; if you need help at any time, press the F1 key. When prompted for an uninstall disk, insert one of the blank disks into drive A; you may need only one disk. When the upgrade process is finished, remove the floppy disks and press Enter. MS-DOS 6 is now installed on your hard disk.

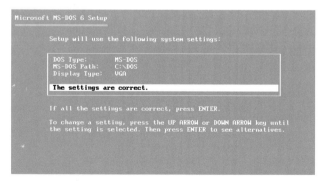

Installing MS-DOS 6 from Scratch

1 With your PC turned off, insert the MS-DOS 6 Setup Disk 1 into drive A. Then switch on your PC, and it will load MS-DOS from the floppy disk rather than the hard disk, which will take a few minutes. Once you see the command line prompt A:\>, you can continue by typing SETUP at the command line.

2 You're now at the same place as step 2 in the previous section on upgrading MS-DOS. The Setup program starts to run and instructions are displayed on screen to guide you through the process. If you need any help, press the F1 key at any time.

You will not be prompted for an uninstall disk, so no blank floppy disks are needed when you install MS-DOS from scratch on a new system. When the process is finished, remove any floppy disks from drive A and restart your PC by pressing the Ctrl, Alt, and Delete keys at the same time. Your PC is now ready to use.

Installing a Mouse on Your PC

When you add a mouse to your PC, you need to install a special software program so that MS-DOS can control it. This program is called a driver. The mouse driver is usually placed in the DOS directory and a special line is added to your CONFIG.SYS file so that the driver gets loaded into memory when you start your PC.

New mice typically come with a floppy disk containing the driver program and installation instructions. Some software programs (such as Microsoft Windows) automatically sense your mouse and activate software to make it run properly.

Other programs require a line such as DEVICE=C:\DOS\ MOUSE.SYS to be inserted in the CONFIG.SYS file. If you have to modify this file, you must restart your PC afterward.

Software Guide

M S-DOS INCLUDES SEVERAL USEFUL PROGRAMS to help you manage your computer, but to use your PC for other functions — such as writing letters, making calculations, combining pictures and text, setting up a database, or playing games — you will need to buy and install extra software. Here is a brief introduction to other available types of software that could considerably expand the capabilities of your computer.

Microsoft Windows

One of the most useful additions you can buy is Microsoft Windows, which offers a very visual "Graphical User Interface" and several helpful programs. With Windows, you can start programs and control the actions mainly with a mouse, so there are very few commands to remember and type in. Windows still requires MS-DOS

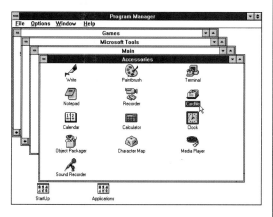

in order to run, but it replaces the command line. Many new PCs are now being sold with Windows already loaded — programs written especially for it will not work without Windows. You can also still run any of your MS-DOS programs from within Windows.

Unlike MS-DOS, Microsoft Windows can do several things at once. It can even run several programs at the same time. Each program is displayed within its own frame, which is called a window. You can have several of these windows open at the same time and switch between them very quickly and easily. Note that many MS-DOS utilities — such as the Anti-Virus and Backup utilities — can also be run from within Windows.

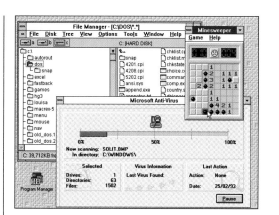

Juggling Programs
In the Windows screen shown here, three different programs are being run at once — a games program, a file management program, and the Anti-Virus program.

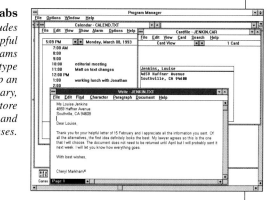

Keeping Tabs
Windows includes a few helpful basic programs that let you type letters, keep an electronic diary, and even store names and addresses.

Pictorial Help
Windows makes your PC much easier to use by representing programs as little pictures, which are called icons.

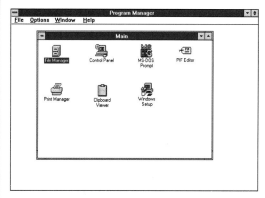

Taking Stock
Individual Windows programs and utilities are arranged in groups, and their icons can be displayed in a group window. The Main *group window is shown above. The* File Manager *program displays, and helps you to organize, the contents of all your directories. With* Print Manager, *you can find out what is happening with any page you have sent to print.*

Word Processing

Early word processing software allowed your PC to be used like a sophisticated typewriter. Today, word processors can do much more. You can type in a letter or report, and then easily change words or move blocks of text around. Word processing programs will also count your words and even check spelling against a huge electronic dictionary.

Some word processing programs work under MS-DOS; others are Windows-based. A program that runs under MS-DOS usually lets you change the typeface or style of your text — for example, to produce bold or italic text. But you cannot see immediately from the image on the monitor how these changes will affect the look of your document when it is printed.

Range of Options
An MS-DOS word processing program typically displays a range of menu options below the typing area, together with information about your cursor's exact location in the text.

Page Preview
Some MS-DOS word processing programs include a page preview mode. Page preview gives you the chance to see exactly how the printed page will look, with different typefaces and type styles.

Windows word processing software, such as Microsoft Word for Windows, allows you the same functions as an MS-DOS program but lets you see exactly how your document will look as you create it on the screen. This feature is called WYSIWYG (what you see is what you get). Because Windows-based word processing programs are designed to be controlled by a mouse, they are especially easy to use. For example, if you want to italicize a section of text, just select the text with your mouse and then click on the italic button at the top of the screen. The program's WYSIWYG capability lets you check everything before you print.

Finished View
Microsoft Word for Windows lets you see on the screen exactly how the text will look — before it is actually printed.

Spreadsheets

PC users who need to do a lot of calculations or financial planning often use a spreadsheet program. A spreadsheet is made up of cells — which can number many thousands — arranged in a grid. Each cell can contain a number, some text, or a formula. A formula can refer to other cells within the spreadsheet.

When you change the contents of a cell, the contents of other cells that are linked to it also change. For example, on a mortgage calculation, you might type into one cell the amount that you want to borrow. A formula entered into another cell would use this number to calculate the monthly payments. You could then alter the amount you wanted to borrow, and the monthly payments would be re-calculated automatically.

Most spreadsheet programs also include charting features, with tools that allow you to plot the values stored in rows or columns as a graph or chart.

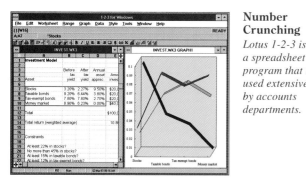

Graphics

You can turn your PC into an easel if you run a paint or drawing program. With the aid of your mouse, you can draw shapes and then fill them with different colors to produce an illustration or a logo.

For complex visual work, you can use a specialized graphics program that lets you create a shape and then stretch it to the correct proportion. Desktop publishing programs aid in the design of page layouts for publication. Text and pictures can be moved about on screen until the right layout is achieved.

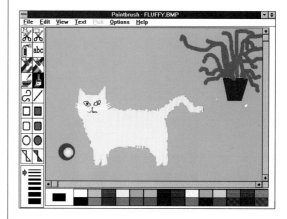

Artistic Device
Windows includes a simple but versatile paint program called Paintbrush that lets you draw on screen using your mouse. You can select different colors from a palette and choose from a variety of brush shapes and other painting and drawing tools — including a "spray can."

Databases

While word processing and spreadsheet programs are helpful for presenting and manipulating information, database programs are useful for storing, sorting, and retrieving data.

If you have many records of invoices or orders, you can manage them better by using a database program. Database software lets you enter new information, search through the data you have stored already, or print out records.

Librarians often use databases to keep track of whether a particular book is on the shelf or out with a reader. A corporation may keep databases about its various products, suppliers, employees, and customers. Doctors may keep databases about patients and their individual medical histories.

You can also ask a database program to search through all the records stored on disk to find a particular one. Or you can ask for a listing of all records with a particular feature in common. Much time and effort can be saved because it takes a database program only a few seconds to search through all the entries recorded.

Record Recovery
A database program such as Microsoft Access will let you design electronic entry forms on your screen. Adding new records, and retrieving them later, is quick and efficient.

Fine Tuning
With CorelDRAW! you can add graduated shades or shadows and work with a wide range of colors and drawing tools.

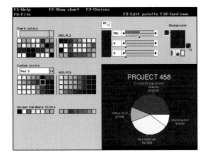

Good Impression
Harvard Graphics 3 lets you create colorful slides. It provides a standard template to which you can add varied graphs or words that emphasize whatever points you want to make in a presentation.

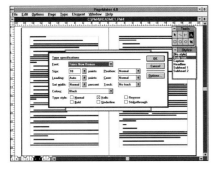

Design Aid
For complex page layouts, you will need desktop publishing (DTP) software, such as Aldus PageMaker. Many magazines and books are now created electronically using DTP software.

Shape Your Text
QuarkXPress 3.1 for Windows offers a flexible and easy way to create pages for publication. Text can be wrapped around images, allowing the user to design interesting and creative layouts.

Communications

Many PC users need to communicate with other users through their respective machines. Any two computers that have serial ports can be linked by means of a special cable called a null-modem cable. The two users can then share data or programs or leave messages with each other by means of the link.

Different computer systems can also communicate with each other over phone lines by using a modem. Communications programs, such as Odyssey, let you call up a remote PC by telephone. You can then have access to a variety of the most up-to-date information stored on that computer — such as current stock prices, weather reports, sports scores, train times, or other data.

Telephone Link
Communications software, such as Odyssey, allows you to transmit data over a telephone by using a modem.

Microsoft Mail is used by workgroups of PC users who are joined in a network. The group can send electronic notes to each other by means of a Workgroup Postoffice (WGPO) with one person acting as an administrator. Each Mail user has his own confidential message file where stored messages are accessed, much like a private mailbox.

Mail Inbox
Messages and folders are listed for each user of Microsoft Mail. A personal password must be used to access messages.

Electronic Mail
Electronic mail programs, such as Microsoft Mail, let you send mail messages to people within your firm's network — even if they are halfway across the world.

Microsoft Mail makes sending messages to large groups of selected people very easy. You use an Address Book to direct your messages and you can even create a personal group name for a number of people to whom the same sort of message should be sent. Whenever you put the group name on a message recipient list, everyone in the group will receive the same communication.

Games and Education

A huge variety of entertaining games and educational software is also available for your PC. You can tackle complex puzzles, fight off space aliens, save the planet from imminent environmental catastrophe, or even help your child learn to read — all on your PC. Many games are best played using a joystick to control actions on the screen. To use one you need a special games port that is included on an expansion card. Be warned that some games are seriously addictive!

You vs Nature
In Superfly!, you take on swarms of flies and other insects — hitting them with a swatter before they can attack.

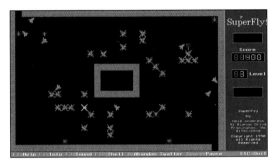

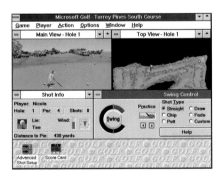

Sporting Chance
Microsoft Golf challenges one or several players to travel around a course attempting to break par through skillful choice of shot type and swing.

Integrated Packages

You might want to use a variety of software on your PC — for example, to use information created in a spreadsheet or database in a chart and then put it into a written report that is passed to someone else on your PC network. Integrated software packages make this all much easier by grouping together programs that offer distinct services but share similar commands — and the cost is usually lower than buying the software programs separately. A disadvantage can be that the components in an integrated package are not as powerful or versatile as separate components.

Installing Software

Follow the "read me first" instructions with the software package. This usually involves putting a disk marked "Disk 1" or "Installation" in a floppy disk drive.

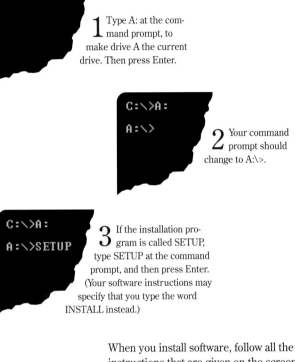

1 Type A: at the command prompt, to make drive A the current drive. Then press Enter.

2 Your command prompt should change to A:\>.

3 If the installation program is called SETUP, type SETUP at the command prompt, and then press Enter. (Your software instructions may specify that you type the word INSTALL instead.)

When you install software, follow all the instructions that are given on the screen and answer any questions you are asked. Eventually the setup program will report that the software has been installed. Once installation is over, you will often be given the program's name or an abbreviation, which you should type at the command prompt to launch the program. You are then ready to go!

Tips for Buying Software

If you take the trouble to buy the right software, life with your PC can be improved considerably.

▓ Think about what tasks you want your PC to perform. Knowing your personal needs helps you to pinpoint the software that will be best for you.

▓ Be sure the software you are considering will run on your computer. Read the software box to determine the hardware and software requirements, noting especially the minimum memory requirements.

▓ Try out any software you are considering if at all possible to see if you will find it friendly to use.

MS-DOS and Memory

MEMORY EXISTS IN THE FORM of chips on your PC's motherboard. All programs need memory to run. When you use a program, MS-DOS loads the program, and any files you want to work with, into random access memory (RAM). When you save a file, MS-DOS copies it from memory to disk. When you want to work on the file again, MS-DOS will load it back into memory because you cannot manipulate information from a disk.

Memories are Made of This

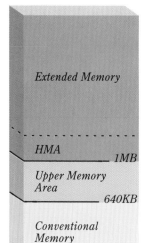

The first 640 kilobytes (KB) of a PC's memory is known as conventional memory, and this is where MS-DOS and all MS-DOS-based programs are run. Above this is the upper memory area, which is used by MS-DOS to control your system's hardware.

Memory beyond 1 megabyte (MB) is known as extended memory; MS-DOS can't use this, but it is used by Windows and Windows-based programs. The first 64KB of extended memory is called the high memory area (HMA).

Type MEM at the command prompt to see what form your PC's memory takes.

MAXIMIZING MEMORY

Normally, MS-DOS uses about 40KB of conventional memory, while device drivers — the special software that drives devices like CD-ROM players or a mouse — may use up another 60 to 100KB. This leaves about 500KB of memory free for applications. Some programs require more than this and will not run because there isn't enough conventional memory free.

However, MS-DOS 6 provides a special utility that will free conventional memory by moving parts of MS-DOS from conventional memory into the high memory area. You can make use of this feature if your PC uses an 80286, 80386, 80486, or the new Pentium processor and you have extended memory installed (use the MEM command to check this).

```
C:\>MEM

Memory Type      Total =  Used  +  Free
----------------------------------------
Conventional      640K    258K     382K
Upper               0K      0K       0K
Adapter RAM/ROM   384K    384K       0K
Extended (XMS)   3072K   3072K       0K
----------------------------------------
Total memory     4096K   3714K     382K

Total under 1 MB  640K    258K     382K

Largest executable program size     382K
Largest free upper memory block       0K

C:\>
```

Size and Type
Use the MEM command to see how the memory in your PC is distributed.

Moving MS-DOS to Higher Memory

You move parts of MS-DOS by using the MS-DOS Editor to alter the CONFIG.SYS file stored in your root directory.

1 Type EDIT CONFIG.SYS at the command prompt and press Enter.

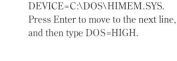
`C:\>EDIT CONFIG.SYS`

```
DEVICE=C:\DOS\SETVER.EXE
FILES=70
BUFFERS=30
STACKS=9,256
SHELL=C:\DOS\COMMAND.COM C:\DOS\   /p
DEVICEHIGH=C:\DOS\DBLSPACE.SYS /MOVE
DEVICE=C:\DOS\HIMEM.SYS
DOS=HIGH
```

2 Use the direction keys to scroll down to the first free line in the file and type the following: DEVICE=C:\DOS\HIMEM.SYS. Press Enter to move to the next line, and then type DOS=HIGH.

```
 File  Edit  Sear
 New
 Open...
 Save
 Save As...

 Print...

 Exit
```

3 Choose *Save* from the *File* menu, and then exit the Editor.

Now restart your PC by pressing the Ctrl, Alt, and Delete keys at the same time. Type in the MEM command again. You will see from the information on your screen that you have more free conventional memory because MS-DOS has been moved into extended memory.

MEMMAKER

Another way of freeing conventional memory is to run the MemMaker program, which puts device drivers into unused areas of upper memory. But note that running MemMaker can result in less free extended memory. You might not need to run it if you use only Windows and Windows-based applications.

To run the MemMaker program, type MEMMAKER at the command prompt and press Enter. Choose the Express Setup option and follow the instructions.

Upgrading Memory

You can improve the performance of Windows and Windows-based programs by adding RAM chips (memory chips) onto your PC's motherboard. Chips can be added either individually or through an expansion card containing banks of RAM chips. This job is best left to an expert.

Batch Files

A BATCH FILE is a simple program file that you can write yourself. The aim is to simplify computer tasks you do often — like running programs — by putting a number of commands together in a single file. You can then start this file with only one or a few keystrokes, and it will automatically execute all the commands stored in it. Batch files also help you to work more accurately. Once you create a batch file and check that it is correct, you remove the risk of making a mistake, as often happens when you type in a long string of commands.

Writing a Batch File

Here is a brief introduction to batch files and how to create them. The example below will run a program and includes basic instructions on which you can expand. Because a batch file is a text file, you can use the Editor to create it.

STEPS TO CREATING YOUR FILE
This batch file will run the Windows program stored in the WINDOWS directory. If you don't have Windows on your PC, substitute the name of a program you do have that you would like to launch from the command prompt. Start the MS-DOS Editor by following the steps on page 68.

1 A batch file mimics the user typing in commands at the command prompt. The first command to type into the batch file will move you to the C drive from any other drive. Type in C: then press Enter to move to the next line.

2 The next command will move you from the current directory of the C drive to the directory containing the program you want to launch. Type CD followed by a space, a backslash, and then the name of the directory. In our example, the directory is WINDOWS.

3 Press Enter to move the insertion point to the next line. The third command will start the program. In our example, the program file is named WIN. Check what yours is called, then type in its name. Press Enter to move to the next line.

4 The final command takes you out of the directory containing the program and returns you to the root directory. Type the fourth line CD \.

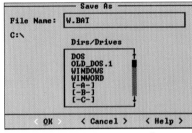

5 Save the batch file in the root directory using the first letter of the program name, followed by the extension BAT. You can now exit from the Editor. Next time you want to run the program, you don't have to change to the correct directory at the command prompt and then type in the program's title. Instead, just type the first letter of the program name (W in our example) and press Enter.

PROGRAM FILE EXTENSIONS
Always be sure to use the extension BAT for a batch file, and never use it for ordinary files that you create. The BAT extension tells MS-DOS that the file is a batch file — that is, it contains special instructions that tell the computer to run a specific program.

Special Commands

Besides using standard MS-DOS commands, batch files can also contain batch commands, which instruct MS-DOS to carry out certain tasks. The following commands can be used in any batch file, including the AUTOEXEC.BAT file that is automatically run every time you turn on your PC (see "Two Special Files" on pages 88 and 89 for more information about this file).

CALL will instruct MS-DOS to run another batch file from the current batch file.

CHOICE will pause the batch file and display a prompt so that you can select an option; you use specified keys to inform MS-DOS of your selection.

ECHO, followed by a message such as "starting program," means that this message will automatically be displayed on the screen when you run the batch file. The message is literally "echoed" on the monitor screen.

GOTO directs MS-DOS to a specific line within the batch file. You must then give this line a "label" so that MS-DOS can recognize it.

PAUSE can be inserted on any line in a batch file to temporarily stop the execution of the file. You can then press any key to make it continue.

What Is a Network?

NETWORKING IS A PRODUCTIVE AND USEFUL WAY to utilize a group of computers. If all of the machines are linked together through a network, you can share an expensive printer, pass files from one PC to another, and even send messages to another user. When a group of computers is connected together in an office, it is known as a *local area network*, or LAN for short.

Using a Network

Moving a file to another PC on a network often involves accessing a network drive, which is a disk drive on another PC — often a large computer that is not used by any one individual but acts as a *file server* for all the other PCs. To use a network drive, you must have a network adapter card in your PC and a network cable plugged into the back of the adapter card.

To access the network, you typically need to "log in" via the command prompt. This is normally done by typing either LOGIN or NET LOGIN, and pressing Enter. You are usually then prompted for your login name and personal password. The network drive has a letter, such as drive F, and you use this drive as if it were actually on your own PC, even though the files are actually stored on the file server's hard disk.

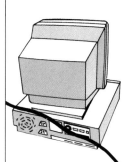

Connecting Link
Special hardware, which includes a network card and connecting cables, must be used to physically link several computers on a network.

CRASH!
Networks can and often do "crash," which sounds devastating but simply means that the file server PC has failed for some reason. When this happens, you can continue using your PC's hard disk but you cannot access the files held on the file server or use the network printer. Once the problem is solved and the main server PC has returned to service, you will need to log back onto it.

Why Have a Network?

The three basic advantages of networking are:

▒ Files can be exchanged without leaving your individual workstation. You don't need to copy files onto floppy disks in order to move them from one PC to another.

▒ Common programs or data files can be run by having a large computer acting as a file server. This machine acts as a large disk drive, holding programs that everyone else can use. Note that this file server doesn't need to be in the same room as the PC users. After logging onto the network, all connected PCs can then have access to the shared information, opening files as needed.

▒ Resources are shared by having common hardware that a number of computers on the network can use. This is a good way to share one expensive laser printer, allowing each PC to produce better hard copies than would be possible if a separate, less expensive printer had to be bought for each individual workstation.

A LAN
An example of a LAN arrangement is shown here. Users of PCs 1 through 4 can save to and retrieve files from the large file server (PC 5), and all computers can print via the network printer.

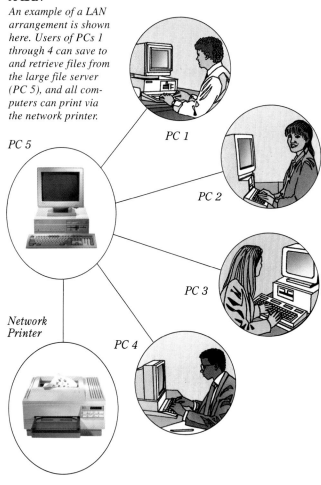

PC 5

PC 1

PC 2

PC 3

PC 4

Network Printer

MS-DOS Commands

A WIDE RANGE OF COMMANDS may be used with MS-DOS 6. Here is a review of the ones you are likely to use most often. The first section lists commands that are entered after the command prompt; the second section (on page 122) lists commands used in batch files or in the CONFIG.SYS file. Always remember to put a space between a command and whatever you type in afterward. If you make a mistake, use the Backspace key to erase it.

At the Command Prompt

CHDIR OR CD Use CD on its own to display the name of the drive and directory in which you are currently located. Typing CD and then the pathname of another directory will allow you to change to that directory; to return to the root directory, type CD and follow it with a backslash.

CHKDSK Use CHKDSK to check the status of a floppy or hard disk. MS-DOS will tell you the amount of used and available disk space, how many files are on the disk, and if any portions of the disk are damaged. If CHKDSK does report that something is wrong, type the command again, but this time follow it with a space and then the switch /f, which instructs MS-DOS to try to fix any errors it can. Press Y at any questions asked.

CLS Use the CLS command to clear the screen and move the command prompt to the top left-hand corner.

COPY The COPY command is used to copy one or more files to the same directory, or to another directory, or to another disk. After the COPY command, type in the full pathname of the file you want to copy, then type in the pathname of the directory to which you want to copy it. If you want to duplicate a file within the same directory, you must give the copy a different name from the original.

DATE DATE gives you the date as recorded by the PC's internal calendar. You can correct it if it is wrong.

DEFRAG The DEFRAG command will start the defragmentation program that optimizes the use of space on a disk by rearranging your files. Be sure to make a backup of important files before you run this program.

DEL Typing DEL followed by the name of a file (or group of files, if you use a wildcard with the command) deletes the file, freeing more space on your hard disk or a floppy disk.

DELTREE If you want to delete a directory and all the files and subdirectories within it, use the DELTREE command followed by the name of the directory.

DIR Typing DIR displays a listing of all the files and subdirectories that are stored in the current directory. If you specify another directory, you can see the files stored in that directory. You can see the contents of another disk if you type the disk drive letter, followed by a colon, after this command.

DISKCOPY This command allows you to duplicate the contents of a floppy disk on another floppy disk. The target disk can be formatted or unformatted, but it must be the same size and capacity as the original disk.

DOSKEY DOSKEY loads the Doskey program into your PC's memory. This program will recall MS-DOS commands and lets you edit anything that you enter at the command prompt.

DBLSPACE Type this command to start the DoubleSpace disk compression program, which can be used to free space on either a hard or floppy disk.

DOSSHELL This starts the MS-DOS Shell, a graphical environment that lets you choose options from drop-down menus. The program can be used as an alternative to the command line if you have trouble remembering commands.

EDIT Use this command to gain access to the MS-DOS Editor program stored in the DOS directory. This rudimentary word processing program can be used to create and edit text files.

FIND Typing the FIND command instructs MS-DOS to look for a specific string of text in a file or files.

FORMAT You use this command to format a floppy disk for use with MS-DOS. After FORMAT, type in the name of the disk drive that contains the disk that you want to format, followed by a colon. Use the switch /q to do a "quick" format on a floppy disk that has previously been formatted. This command can be used only with drive A or B.

HELP If you cannot remember what a command does, type HELP and then the command; an explanation will appear on your screen.

INTERLNK Using the INTERLNK command after connecting your desktop PC to a laptop allows the transfer of files between the two computers and lets them share printer ports.

MEM The MEM command displays the amount of used and free memory in your computer and tells you what form this memory takes and the type that is available for use.

MEMMAKER Type this command to start the MemMaker program, which frees more of a PC's conventional memory by loading device drivers into the upper memory area. MemMaker is for those who use mainly MS-DOS applications; if you use only Windows programs, you may not need to run it.

MKDIR OR MD When you want to create a new directory on a disk, type MKDIR or MD followed by the name of the directory you want to create.

MORE Using MORE lets you view large text files one screenful at a time. This command must be followed by a space, then a less-than character (<), another space, and finally the name of the file you want to view.

MOVE This command moves a file or files from one directory to another. After MOVE, you type in the name of the file you want to move and then the directory you want to move it to. You can also use the MOVE command to rename files and directories.

MSAV Typing MSAV at the command prompt starts the MS-DOS Anti-Virus program, which scans your disks to see if there are any known viruses present. If any viruses are discovered, they will be eliminated by the MSAV program.

MSBACKUP MSBACKUP is the command used to start Microsoft Backup, a program that simplifies the task of backing up data, whether this consists of a single file, a directory, or the entire contents of a hard disk. The COPY command is useful if the material to be copied will fit on one floppy disk; but for large amounts of data, use MSBACKUP. This command can also be used to restore a file to the hard disk.

PRINT This command lets you print a copy of a file containing unformatted text.

PROMPT This command changes the appearance of your command prompt for the duration of a work session. Typing PROMPT followed by $P and pressing Enter creates a command prompt that shows your disk drive and directory; to show the greater-than (>) character, type $G. So typing PG after the PROMPT command will give you the standard command prompt. To change the look of your prompt permanently, you need to alter the prompt line in your AUTOEXEC.BAT file (see page 89 for more information).

 RENAME OR REN Using REN or RENAME will change a filename without changing the contents of the file. After typing REN, you type the name of the file you want to rename and then follow this with the file's new name.

RESTORE The RESTORE command lets you copy files that were backed up to a disk with the BACKUP command available in previous versions of MS-DOS — that is, versions prior to MS-DOS 6.

 RMDIR OR RD The RMDIR or RD command deletes a directory. Before you can remove a directory, you must empty the directory of its files and subdirectories (see also DELTREE).

TIME The TIME command displays the current time according to the PC's internal clock. You can change the time if you want; if the time shown is correct, just press Enter.

TREE The TREE command is used to display the complete directory tree structure beneath the current directory. If used in a disk's root directory it displays the whole structure of that disk.

 TYPE The TYPE command lets you view the contents of a text file on your screen (see also MORE). You type the filename after the TYPE command.

UNDELETE Using the UNDELETE command lets you regain a file that was previously deleted using the DEL command. For the best chance of success, use this command as soon as possible after accidentally deleting a file.

VER Use the VER command to display the current version number of MS-DOS that is installed on your PC.

VSAFE This command sets up a program that continuously monitors your PC for viruses. If one is found, a warning will be displayed on the monitor.

XCOPY The XCOPY command is similar to COPY, but faster. It is used to copy directories and subdirectories.

MS-DOS Commands Used in System Files

The following commands can be used to modify your CONFIG.SYS file or to initiate actions in batch programs.

DEVICE Used in the CONFIG.SYS file, this command will load a specified device driver — a software program that controls a peripheral — into memory.

ECHO A special command used in batch files, any text that you type after this command will be displayed on the screen when you run the program.

PATH The PATH command goes into the AUTOEXEC.BAT file and defines a search path along which MS-DOS will look for a program that you ask it to run.

PAUSE When entered in a batch file, PAUSE displays a message prompting the user to press any key before the program continues.

Error Messages

A VARIETY OF ERROR MESSAGES may appear on the screen when you use your computer. The words may seem abrupt and alarming — but the causes are usually just simple mistakes that can be put right by retracing your steps. For example, check that floppy disks are in the right drives, that drive doors are shut, and that you have typed instructions exactly as you intended.

POST Error Messages

Incorrect configuration data in CMOS Your PC has preset options, which are recorded on the motherboard. During the power-on self-test (POST) when you switch on, this data is compared with the settings of the components in your system. If a discrepancy is detected, the above error message appears. It might also be displayed during startup after you install more memory or change your system hardware. To correct the settings, call a technician to run the setup utility on your computer.

No boot device available This message indicates that your PC's hard disk may have been damaged. Switch off your PC, wait a few seconds, and then switch it on again. If the same message appears, call a technician. Your PC's hard disk or its controller is damaged and you may need to replace one or both.

MS-DOS Messages

Access denied You have tried to change or delete a file that MS-DOS does not allow you to change or that someone has protected. If this is causing a serious problem, ask for an expert's opinion on what can be done.

Bad command or file name The command you have just typed is not understood by MS-DOS. First check that you have spelled it correctly. If you have asked MS-DOS to run a program, check that the program is installed and that you are in the correct directory.

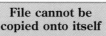 **Duplicate file name** You've used the REN command to rename a file, but the new name duplicates the name of a file that already exists. Decide on a different name for the file you want to rename, and then retype the command.

File cannot be copied onto itself You have made an error with the COPY command. Check that you haven't specified a filename twice.

File not found You have just made the very easy mistake of typing a command for a file that does not exist. First check that you have used the correct spelling and wording — and then try again.

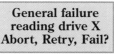 **General failure reading drive X Abort, Retry, Fail?** This message usually means that you have asked MS-DOS to access the contents of a floppy disk and it cannot do so. This may be because the floppy disk has not yet been formatted. Other possible causes are that the floppy disk is faulty or that you are trying to read a high-capacity floppy disk in a low-capacity drive. Try inserting a different disk that you know is formatted and has the same capacity as the floppy disk drive. Press R for Retry. If that doesn't work, press A for Abort. If that still does not help, restart the computer.

Insufficient disk space If a hard disk or floppy disk is full, you may see this message on the screen. You can either choose another disk that contains more free space or delete data that you no longer need from the disk you were trying to use.

Invalid drive specification This message appears when you type an instruction involving a drive letter that is not accessible from your PC. Check that you have typed the correct drive letter followed by a colon.

Invalid parameter or Invalid switch This error message may appear if you mistype an instruction at the command prompt. Type your instruction again.

Non-System disk or disk error If you see this message, it means you must have tried to start up your PC after leaving a floppy disk in drive A. The PC has looked at this floppy disk to see if it contains MS-DOS and has not found it. Be sure drive A contains no floppy disk and then press any key so that MS-DOS will start up from the hard disk drive.

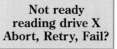 **Not ready reading drive X Abort, Retry, Fail?** This message indicates that you have tried to access one of your floppy disk drives but have forgotten to put in a disk first or have left the door open. Insert a disk, close the latch, then press R for Retry.

Path not found You may see this message if you specify a directory that doesn't exist. Check the validity of your command.

 Too many parameters This means that you have included too many parts in a command, or mistyped the command, possibly including an extra space you should not have. Check the validity of your command and try again.

Write protect error writing drive X Abort, Retry, Fail? You have tried to write to or alter a floppy disk that has been write-protected. Take out the disk, remove the write protection (if you no longer need it), insert the disk again, and press R for Retry. Alternatively, use a different disk and press R for Retry.

My PC Doesn't Work

OCCASIONALLY YOUR COMPUTER may not do exactly what you expect or nothing may happen when you switch on. If you find yourself at a complete standstill, follow the diagram below to trace the problem. You may need to call professional help — but often the cause is something that you can put right yourself very easily. First make routine checks that cords, cables, switches, and disk drives are as they should be — and that nothing is accidentally resting on your keyboard.

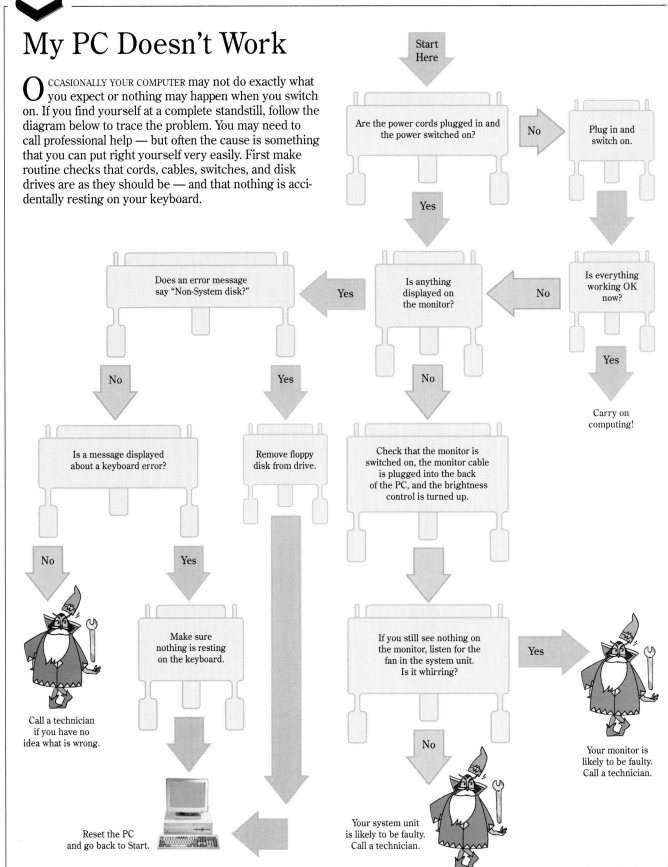

Start Here

Are the power cords plugged in and the power switched on?

No → Plug in and switch on.

Yes ↓

Does an error message say "Non-System disk?" ← **Yes** ← Is anything displayed on the monitor? ← **No** ← Is everything working OK now?

Yes ↓

Carry on computing!

No ↓ / **Yes** ↓ / **No** ↓

Is a message displayed about a keyboard error?

Remove floppy disk from drive.

Check that the monitor is switched on, the monitor cable is plugged into the back of the PC, and the brightness control is turned up.

No ↓ / **Yes** ↓

Make sure nothing is resting on the keyboard.

If you still see nothing on the monitor, listen for the fan in the system unit. Is it whirring?

Yes → Your monitor is likely to be faulty. Call a technician.

No ↓

Your system unit is likely to be faulty. Call a technician.

Call a technician if you have no idea what is wrong.

Reset the PC and go back to Start.

GLOSSARY

In this glossary, terms in italics refer to other items in the glossary.

a **Application**
A type of computer *program*, such as a spreadsheet, word processing, or database program.

ASCII
A term applied to *files* containing simple, unformatted text; the ASCII "code" is a set of 128 numbers representing letters, numbers, and symbols.

b **Batch file**
A *program* that you can write yourself to simplify computer tasks you do often.

Bit
A switch within a computer containing the value 0 or 1. Eight bits make a *byte*.

Booting
Turning on a computer and loading MS-DOS.

Byte
A unit of information within a computer, made up of eight *bits*. Different byte values correspond to different letters and numerals.

c **Cache memory**
Fast, expensive *memory* added to your PC to speed up processing or storage of *files*.

CD-ROM
Compact Disc Read-Only Memory, a storage medium for large amounts of *data*.

Central Processing Unit
The electronic component within the *system unit* that acts as the computer's control center and the place where instructions are performed.

Chip
A small piece of silicon on which an integrated circuit has been formed.

Command
An instruction to the computer's *CPU* or to *MS-DOS* to do something.

Command line
Instructions typed at the *command prompt*.

Command prompt
A group of characters (most often C:\>) on the monitor screen that "prompts" you to type a command to *MS-DOS*.

CPU
Central processing unit.

Crash
A standstill in the operation of a computer, due to an error.

Current directory
The *directory* you are in or using at present.

d **Data**
Information, whether in the form of text, numbers, or images, stored on a computer.

Default
The standard option that is set automatically.

Digital
A term referring to the use of digits to represent *data*.

Directory
A group of *files* on a disk.

Disk
A *hard disk* or *floppy disk*.

Disk drive
The unit that rotates a *disk* and reads or writes *data* or *programs* from it.

Display adapter card
An *expansion card* plugged into the *motherboard*; enables information to appear on the monitor screen.

Dot pitch
The diameter of each dot forming an image on the monitor screen.

e **Electronic mail**
The sending of messages between users on a *network*.

Expansion bus
A group of wires carrying *data* between the *CPU* and the *expansion slots*.

Expansion card
A card that is fitted into an *expansion slot*. Expansion cards extend a PC's capabilities — for example, by linking it to a *network*.

Expansion slot
A slot at the back of the *motherboard* that provides electrical connectors for fitting an *expansion card*.

Extension
A three-character addition to the name of a *file*, describing its type.

f **File**
A named collection of *data*, or a *program*, stored on a *disk*.

File server
The main computer on a *network*, usually the fastest and with the largest *hard disk*, used to store *files* shared by other PCs.

Floppy disk
A magnetically-coated, portable plastic disk, used for storing or transferring *data* and *programs*.

Formatting
The laying down of markers on a *disk*; allows *MS-DOS* to find and retrieve *files*.

g **Graphical User Interface (GUI)**
Software that allows the user to control the computer in an intuitive way through choosing pictures or symbols that represent *programs* or *commands*.

h **Hardware**
The physical equipment used in computing.

Hard disk
A magnetically-coated disk within the *system unit*; used for permanent storage of *data* and *programs*; stores more data than a *floppy disk*.

Icon
A picture on the monitor screen that can represent a *program* or other option.

Kilobyte (KB)
Approximately 1,000 bytes (1,024 to be exact).

Local area network (LAN)
A relatively small *network*.

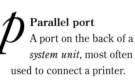

Megabyte (MB)
Approximately one million *bytes*.

Memory
Chips in a computer where *data* is stored temporarily when it is being worked on and when *programs* are being run (*RAM* or random access memory); or where some basic information concerning the operation of a computer is stored (*ROM* or read-only memory).

Menu
A range of options or *commands*, displayed on the monitor screen, from which you can choose.

Microprocessor
The *central processing unit*.

Modem
A device that can convert electronic information from a computer into sounds for transmission over telephone lines, or vice-versa.

Motherboard
A fiberglass board in a *system unit* on which the electronic components are mounted.

Mouse
A hand-held device used to point to and manipulate items on the monitor screen.

MS-DOS
Microsoft Disk Operating System; the most popular *operating system* for PCs.

MS-DOS Shell
An easy-to-use graphical version of *MS-DOS*.

Multimedia
Information presented or stored in a combination of forms, using graphics, text, sound, and animation.

Network
A number of computers linked together so they can share *files* and *hardware*.

Online
Switched on and ready.

Operating system
A *program* that controls a computer's *hardware* and handles interactions between the operator, the *software*, and the hardware.

Parallel port
A port on the back of a *system unit*, most often used to connect a printer.

Pathname
A full description of a *file* that includes which *disk drive* the file is on and the series of *directories* that must be passed through from the *root directory* to reach the file.

Peripheral
A piece of hardware attached to a computer that adds to what the computer can do.

Pixel
One of many thousands of units that make up the monitor display, consisting of a dot or group of dots.

Program
A *file* containing instructions for a computer to perform a function or an operation.

RAM
Random access memory; see *memory*.

Resolution
The number of *pixels* that make up a monitor screen image; the more pixels there are, the higher the resolution.

ROM
Read-only memory; see *memory*.

Root directory
The primary *directory* on a *disk*, off which other directories branch.

Serial port
The port on the back of the *system unit* into which a *peripheral* such as a *mouse* or scanner can be plugged.

Software
Programs.

Source
The original *disk* or *directory* from which a *file* or *files* is copied or moved.

Subdirectory
A *directory* that is contained within another directory.

Switch
Something typed after an *MS-DOS command* that modifies the way the command works.

System unit
A box that holds the most important electronic components of a PC.

Target
The destination *disk* or *directory* of a copied or moved *file*.

Upgrading
Making additions to your PC in terms of *hardware*, *software*, and so on.

Virus
A tiny *program* that can copy itself onto a *floppy disk* or *hard disk*, wrecking *files* or corrupting *data*.

Window
A bordered area on a monitor screen where special information is shown.

Windows
A popular *Graphical User Interface* that allows you to run different *programs* simultaneously in different *windows*.

Write-protect
A method of protecting information on a *disk* from being altered or erased.

INDEX

Equipment Suppliers:
Equipment on pages 8-14, 16-17, 21
(top), 22-23, 26, 28, 31, 40, 41, 44-45
appears courtesy of Mesh, London, UK.
The tape backup unit on page 14 is
courtesy of CMS Peripherals, London,
UK, and the palmtop PC on page 15 is
courtesy of Supply Line, London, UK.

Register Today!

Return this
*The Way Computers
and MS-DOS® Work*
registration card for:

✔ information on forthcoming WYSIWYG titles

✔ a Microsoft Press catalog

✔ exclusive offers on specially priced books

Fill in information below and mail postage free. Please mail the bottom half of this page.

Please tear off
this portion
before mailing

NAME

COMPANY

ADDRESS

CITY   STATE   ZIP

Your feedback is important to us.

Include your daytime telephone number and we might call to find out how you use *The Way Computers and MS-DOS Work* and what we can do to make future editions even more useful. If we call you, we'll send you a **FREE GIFT** for your time!

(   )

DAYTIME TELEPHONE NUMBER

Coming Soon!

Let the WYSIWYG Series show you the easy route to mastering Microsoft® Excel for Windows™ and Microsoft Word for Windows.

Return the registration card to Microsoft Press and we'll let you know as soon as these books are available.

The Way Word for Windows™ Works
Peter Gloster

New and occasional users of Microsoft Word for Windows will enjoy this graphical introduction to the software. This is the only book that will actually *show* you with full-color photographs, screen shots, and attractive sample documents the best way to use Microsoft Word for Windows. All the major features of Word for Windows are covered.

128 pages, softcover   8 x 10 $18.95 ($24.95 Canada)   ISBN 1-55615-569-7
Available November 1993

The Way Microsoft® Excel for Windows™ Works
Bryn Clark

This book introduces all major features of Microsoft Excel for Windows— from spreadsheets, charts, and databases through configuration and customization—in a friendly, visual manner. Each section uses the integration of text and graphics to make seemingly complex tasks as easy as the click of a mouse.

128 pages, softcover   8 x 10 $18.95 ($24.95 Canada)   ISBN 1-55615-570-0
Available January 1994

Microsoft Press books are available wherever quality computer books are sold. Or call 1-800-MSPRESS for ordering information.
Outside the U.S., write to International Coordinator, Microsoft Press, One Microsoft Way, Redmond, WA 98052-6399

NO POSTAGE
NECESSARY
IF MAILED
IN THE
UNITED STATES

BUSINESS REPLY MAIL
FIRST-CLASS MAIL   PERMIT NO. 53   BOTHELL, WA

POSTAGE WILL BE PAID BY ADDRESSEE

MICROSOFT PRESS REGISTRATION
THE WAY COMPUTERS AND MS-DOS WORK
PO BOX 3019
BOTHELL WA   98041-9910